HIDDEN GEMS OF AMERICA

WINERIES & VINEYARDS

2019

BEST OF THE BEST WINES

PARENTESI QUADRA

Published by Parentesi Quadra
PQ Publishing
Calle Gr. Esteve
46004, Valencia, Spain

Legal & Disclaimer

The content and information in this book has been provided for educational and entertainment purposes only. The content and information contained in this book has been compiled from sources deemed reliable, and it is accurate to the best of the Author's knowledge, information and belief. However, the Author cannot guarantee its accuracy and validity and cannot be held liable for any errors and/or omissions. Further, changes are periodically made to this book as and when needed, where appropriate and/or necessary.

Limit of liability/disclaimer of warranty: While the Publisher and Author have used their best efforts in preparing this book, they make no representations or warranties with respect to the accuracy and completeness of the contents of this book and specifically disclaim any implied warranties of merchantability of fitness for a particular purpose. No warranty may be created or extended by sales representatives or written sales materials.

Edition IV
Printed in the United States of America

CONTENTS

Editor's Note

Hidden Gems of America – Wineries and Vineyards is passion - passion for good wine. Brought to us by real people who are caring, love what they do and what to do more and better. Each and every day.

Hidden Gems of America is a dream come true. It is like seeing again a beloved friend after many years apart. It is love. Love for good wine.

We have gathered the Best of the Best Wines from coast to coast and north to south. We searched for the gems that were very good investments for the palate; the search was hedonistic and technical. We looked for excellent wines from a technical perspective of wine tasting but also had that special love caring and purpose of the owner. That special touch.

We looked for only the best, regardless of dimension or any other operational scale. Just the best, for you, who we assume would appreciate the best!

With Passion.

Somm. S. Margos

CALLAGHAN VINEYARDS

Elgin, ARIZONA

www.callaghanvineyards.com
E-mail: callaghanvineyards@gmail.com
Address: 336 Elgin Road, Elgin, AZ 85611
Phone: (520) 455-5322

HISTORY

Callaghan Vineyards was founded in 1990 by Karen and Harold Callaghan and their son Kent. The family had no prior experience in the wine business, but Harold had enjoyed a brief period of home winemaking and decided to start a commercial operation. The estate Buena Suerte Vineyard was planted in 1990 in the middle of a vicious heat wave. Sky Harbor Airport in Phoenix had to shut down for a couple of days due to the heat, which also claimed thousands of newly planted vines.

This experience set the stage for the experimentation that would follow over the years. Kent looked for rootstocks and grape varieties best suited to the warm, windy, sun-bleached region that is southeastern Arizona. Over many years, the focus has changed from Bordeaux to the Mediterranean. Graciano, Grenache, Mourvèdre, Tempranillo all figure prominently in Callaghan bottlings. Two Atlantic varieties - Petit Verdot and Tannat - have also excelled in southern Arizona. Callaghan Vineyards was the first to plant all of these varieties in Arizona. Callaghan Vineyards' wines have been served at the White House on four occasions.

OWNERSHIP & MANAGEMENT

Lisa and Kent Callaghan own and operate Callaghan Vineyards. Lisa is the driving force in the tasting room and hospitality aspects of the business. Her warmth, style and personality are integral to the success of Callaghan Vineyards. Kent spends most of his time working in the vineyard, pruning in the winter and working the vines during the growing season. Given the hands off approach in the winery, Kent's winemaking activity is limited to topping barrels, racking barrels twice a year and bottling. Lisa and Kent's marriage is, literally and figuratively, a great one.

WINEMAKER

Winemaker, Kent Callaghan prefers a minimalist approach to winemaking. Other than a great destemmer and a good press, the winery has no fancy equipment. It houses a lot of European oak barrels ranging from new to 15 years old. The guiding philosophy is to produce distinctive, complex and deep wines that reflect the character of the site and the vintage.

VINEYARD

The winery owns 50 acres of land, out of which 25 acres is under vine. The vineyard site is sloped slightly east and also north and south. Multiple exposures are possible depending on the block. Soil composition varies considerably across the vineyard. Red, iron-rich, clay loam predominates, but they also have areas of chalky outcroppings. In general, the soils are unusually high in bicarbonates and low in the nutrients that would give vines vigor and high yields. Given these natural constraints, the vines are smaller and more densely planted than they would be in other areas of Arizona. Yields are among the lowest in Arizona which produces wines of real depth and character.

GRAPES GROWN
- Cabernet Sauvignon
- Graciano
- Mourvèdre
- Merlot
- Petit Verdot
- Tannat
- Tempranillo
- Cabernet Franc
- Other

In their fermentation process they use commercial yeast in most cases. Due to often humid conditions, the grapes can harbor unwanted microbes. Malolactic fermentation, on the other hand, usually occurs spontaneously in the winery. All of the white wines are barrel-fermented with mostly neutral oak, and stay on the lees until bottling. Reds are fermented in 0.5 to 1-ton open top fermenters. Most are de-stemmed, with a majority of whole berries. Punch-downs occur 2 to 3 times daily for the first 3 to 4 days, then once daily as the fermentation subsides.

Callaghan wines are available at the winery and at select restaurants and retailers throughout the state of Arizona.

Top restaurants that serve Callaghan Wines

1. FnB Restaurant, Scottsdale. AZ
2. Beckett's Table, Phoenix, AZ
3. Southern Rail, Phoenix, AZ
4. Binkley's, Phoenix, AZ
5. Feast, Tucson, AZ
6. Wild Garlic, Tucson, AZ
7. Hacienda del Sol, Tucson, AZ
8. AZ Wine Collective, Tucson, AZ

VISITOR INFORMATION
The winery and tasting room can be visited without appointment. Tours and tastings are available at a cost. The winery receives over 15,000 visitors annually.

WINES

Lisa's

Varietals: Viognier (30%), Roussanne (20%), Marsanne (15%), Malvasia Bianca (15%), Clairette (10%), Petit Manseng (10%)
Barrel Aging: 9 months in oak
Type of Wine: White
Alcohol: 13,0%
Optimal Serving Temperature: 55° F
Vintage Year: 2016
Bottle Format: 750ml
Awards: Silver Medal, 2018 San Francisco Chronicle Wine Competition

Rhumb Line Grenache

Varietals: Grenache (100%)
Barrel Aging: 8 months
Skin Contact: 10 days
Type of Wine: Red
Alcohol: 15,0%
Optimal Serving Temperature: 63° F
Vintage Year: 2017
Bottle Format: 750ml
Awards: Silver Medal, 2019 San Francisco Chronicle Wine Competition

Caitlin's

Varietals: Petit Verdot (67%), Cabernet Franc (33%)
Barrel Aging: 18 months in French and Austrian oak; 75% new
Skin Contact: 8 days
Type of Wine: Red
Alcohol: 13,8%
Optimal Serving Temperature: 63° F
Vintage Year: 2016
Bottle Format: 750ml
Awards: Silver Medal, 2019 San Francisco Chronicle Wine Competition; Silver Medal, 2018 Jefferson Cup Competition

Padres

Varietals: Graciano (62%), Cabernet Sauvignon (19%), Tannat (19%)
Barrel Aging: 18 months in French and Austrian oak; 33% new
Skin Contact: 10 days
Type of Wine: Red
Alcohol: 14,8%
Optimal Serving Temperature: 63° F
Vintage Year: 2016
Bottle Format: 750ml
Awards: Gold Medal, 2018 Jefferson Cup Competition

Tannat

Varietals: Tannat (100%)
Barrel Aging: 18 months in French oak; 50% new
Skin Contact: 8 days
Type of Wine: Red
Alcohol: 14,8%
Optimal Serving Temperature: 63° F
Vintage Year: 2016
Bottle Format: 750ml
Awards: Double Gold Medal, 2019 San Francisco Chronicle Wine Competition

Claire's

Varietals: Mourvèdre (65%), Graciano (25%), Petit Verdot (10%)
Barrel Aging: 18 months
Skin Contact: 10 days
Type of Wine: Red
Alcohol: 15,0%
Optimal Serving Temperature: 63° F
Vintage Year: 2016
Bottle Format: 750ml

BIEN NACIDO ESTATE

Santa Maria, CALIFORNIA

www.biennacidoestate.com
E-mail: info@biennacidoestate.com
Address: 2963 Grand Avenue, Suite B,
Los Olivos, CA 93441
Phone: (805) 318-6640

HISTORY

In 1837 Tomas Olivera received a Spanish land grant that stretched from the Santa Maria Mesa to the San Rafael Mountains. He called it Rancho Tepusquet after the nearby creek. His daughter and son-in-law constructed an adobe in 1857 and raised cattle, grain, and wine grapes. Over the years, the heirs of Don Pacifico divided the property and the Rancho diminished.

In 1969, brothers Steve & Bob Miller, the fourth-generation of the Miller Family, purchased two of the land grant's parcels in the Santa Maria Valley and united them as Rancho Tepusquet. The Miller brothers recognized that the soils and climate were ideal for growing premium wine grapes. In the early 1970's they planted the vineyard and christened it Bien Nacido Vineyards meaning "well born." Since that time, Bien Nacido Vineyards has earned the respect of winemakers, critics, and wine consumers. It is a remarkable place which produces premium Pinot Noir, Chardonnay, and Syrah as well as many other varieties.

The Miller Family also planted the Solomon Hills Vineyard in the late 1990's. Known for Pinot Noir and Chardonnay, Solomon Hills found its tenor early on in its relatively young life among a broad range of talented winemakers who found its vibrant, youthful flavor profile exhilarating, and, at times, profound.

Bien Nacido Vineyards' position within the Santa Maria Valley AVA, one of the coolest wine growing climates in America, makes it ideal for growing Burgundian varieties such as Pinot Noir and Chardonnay. The vineyard also produces cool climate expressions of Grenache and Syrah and was the first commercial vineyard in California to plant cool climate Syrah.

Bien Nacido Vineyards has a distinct spirit and a harmony of its own. The winegrowing team has nurtured the vineyard's uniqueness through mindful farming and their commitment to agricultural excellence. Those who make wine from Bien Nacido fruit translate that message into an array of liquid expressions.

OWNERSHIP & MANAGEMENT

The Miller family has been farming California's soil for five generations and has earned respect for their agricultural influence since the late 1800's. The family business is currently operated by Stephen T.B. Miller - CEO/President (Bien Nacido's founder, 4th generation), Marshall Miller - VP Finance & Operations (5th generation) and Nicholas Miller - VP of Sales & Marketing (5th generation).

Due to their hard work, pioneering of quality mechanization in the field and constant dedication to grape quality they were recognized as one of the "Most Admired Grapegrowers in North America" by Vineyard and Winery Management Magazine. The family continues its legacy of agricultural integrity and winemaking innovation year after year.

WINEMAKER

Trey Fletcher joined Bien Nacido Estate in 2011 as Winemaker and General Manager. Trey studied Enology & Viticulture at California State University, Fresno. He has made wine and grown grapes in Europe, New Zealand, Argentina and California. Upon returning to the United States, he has worked several vintages in the Napa Valley, Sonoma Coast and Central Coast of California. Most recently he was Associate Winemaker at Littorai Wines on the Sonoma Coast. Trey's seamless integration of viticulture and winemaking at Bien Nacido drives his focused and intuitive approach.

VINEYARD

Estate Wines focuses on only 37 acres which are believed to produce the best fruit. The terroir is a combination of the rocky soils, cool climate, and ocean influence. It is located on the eastern opening of a transverse mountain range which delivers a steady wash of cool marine air. The soil structure is diverse, made up primarily of sandy loam, chalk, gravelly loam, and marine loam.

All fermentations are native, they do not add yeast. They sort all the fruit and destem a portion depending on the vintage and vineyard location. The wines generally ferment for 3 weeks in open-top fermenters with a mix of punch-downs and pump-overs. They generally press the reds at dryness. The Chardonnay is whole-cluster pressed, and barrel-fermented and aged sur lie.

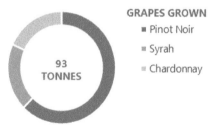

GRAPES GROWN

- Pinot Noir
- Syrah
- Chardonnay

Bien Nacido wines are available via their website and tasting room. The wines are distributed across the United States and are also exported to England, Belgium, Canada, China, Korea, Japan and Germany.

Top restaurants that serve Bien Nacido Wines

1. Single Thread Farm Restaurant, Healdsburg, CA
2. Lazy Bear, San Francisco, CA
3. Aureole, Las Vegas, NV
4. Addison Restaurant, San Diego, CA
5. Pappas Steakhouse-Galleria, Houston, TX
6. Bourbon Steak - Fairmount, Scottsdale, AZ
7. Masseria, Washington, DC
8. Highball & Harvest - Ritz Carlton, Orlando, FL
9. Canoe Club - Montage, Bluffton, SC
10. John Howie Steak, Bellevue, WA

VISITOR INFORMATION

The tasting room can be visited without appointment. Tastings are available at a cost.

WINES

Santa Maria Valley Chardonnay

Varietals: Chardonnay (100%)
Barrel Aging: 18 months in French oak; 25% new
Type of Wine: White
Alcohol: 13%
Optimal Serving Temperature: 50° F
Vintage Year: 2016
Bottle Format: 750ml

Santa Maria Valley Pinot Noir

Varietals: Pinot Noir (100%)
Barrel Aging: 16 months in French oak; 33% new
Skin Contact: 22 days
Type of Wine: Red
Alcohol: 13,0%
Optimal Serving Temperature: 50-55° F
Vintage Year: 2015
Bottle Format: 750ml

Santa Maria Valley Syrah

Varietals: Syrah (98%), Viognier (2%)
Barrel Aging: 16 months in French oak; 20% new
Skin Contact: 23 days
Type of Wine: Red
Alcohol: 13,5%
Optimal Serving Temperature: 65° F
Vintage Year: 2015
Bottle Format: 750ml

Santa Maria Valley The Captain Pinot Noir

Varietals: Pinot Noir (100%)
Barrel Aging: 18 months in French oak; 40% new
Skin Contact: 22 days
Type of Wine: Red
Alcohol: 13,0%
Optimal Serving Temperature: 50-55° F
Vintage Year: 2015
Bottle Format: 750ml

Santa Maria Valley The XO Syrah

Varietals: Syrah (100%)
Barrel Aging: 16 months in French oak; 18% new
Skin Contact: 22 days
Type of Wine: Red
Alcohol: 13%
Optimal Serving Temperature: 65° F
Vintage Year: 2015
Bottle Format: 750ml

Santa Maria Valley LXIII Pinot Noir

Varietals: Pinot Noir (100%)
Barrel Aging: 16 months in French oak; 30% new
Skin Contact: 21 days
Type of Wine: Red
Alcohol: 13,5%
Optimal Serving Temperature: 50-55° F
Vintage Year: 2015
Bottle Format: 750ml

CALERA

Hollister, CALIFORNIA

www.calerawine.com
E-mail: info@calerawine.com
Address: 11300 Cienega Road, Hollister, CA 95023
Phone: (831) 637-9170

HISTORY

In 1975, legendary vintner and American wine pioneer Josh Jensen founded Calera (Spanish for "lime kiln") high in the remote Gavilan Mountains of California's windswept Central Coast. There, in Mt. Harlan's low-yielding, limestone-rich soils and cool, arid climate, he began planting what would ultimately become six small estate vineyards.

Today, these vineyards are recognized as some of the New World's most revered Pinot Noir sites. Under the stewardship of Winemaker Mike Waller, each vineyard is renowned for producing singular wines of uncommon purity, elegance and aging potential. In addition to its beloved single-vineyard wines, Calera partners with some of the top vineyards on California's majestic Central Coast to make Calera's beautiful Central Coast wines, including Pinot Noir, Chardonnay, Viognier and a Vin Gris of Pinot Noir.

OWNERSHIP & MANAGEMENT

Duckhorn Wine Company has set the standard for American fine wine for four decades. The acclaimed Duckhorn Wine Company portfolio includes Duckhorn Vineyards, Paraduxx,

Goldeneye, Migration, Decoy, Canvasback, Calera and Kosta Browne, each with its own dedicated winemaker. With more than 850 acres of renowned estate vineyards, along with grapes from the finest growers, each winery has a canvas of lots from which to blend its wines. Focused on optimal grape selection, innovative winemaking techniques and a premium barrel-aging program, Duckhorn Wine Company is founded on a pioneering spirit and unwavering commitment to quality.

WINEMAKER
A master of Pinot Noir, known for his terroir-driven approach to winemaking, Mike Waller has worked alongside legendary vintner Josh Jensen for more than a decade, helping to guide winemaking at Calera. Mike's winemaking style honors the character and complexity of Calera's six renowned sites on Mt. Harlan, which are the source for some of the New World's most revered wines. In the winery, Mike captures the nuance of these grand cru-caliber vineyards to create sophisticated wines renowned for their layered elegance and aging potential.

VINEYARD
The winery owns 600 acres of land, out of which 83 acres are under vine. The soil type is limestone with decomposed granite top.

In their fermentation process they let their grapes spontaneously ferment without adding any yeast. Mt. Harlan Pinot Noirs are whole-cluster fermented for 2 weeks. Central Coast Pinot Noirs are typically destemmed and fermented for 2 weeks. All white wines are whole-cluster pressed and barrel-fermented.

GRAPES GROWN

- Pinot Noir
- Chardonnay
- Viognier
- Aligote

83
ACRES

121
TONNES

Calera wines are available via their website and the tasting room. The wines are distributed across the United States and the world.

VISITOR INFORMATION
The winery and tasting rooms can be visited without appointment. Tours and tastings are available at a cost. Group tours (maximum 12 people) are also available. The winery receives about 3,000 visitors annually and is also available for private events.

WINES

Jensen

Varietals: Pinot Noir (100%)
Barrel Aging: 18 months in French oak; 30% new
Skin Contact: 14 days
Type of Wine: Red
Alcohol: 14,0%
Optimal Serving Temperature: 60 ˚F
Vintage Year: 2016
Bottle Format: 750ml

Mills

Varietals: Pinot Noir (100%)
Barrel Aging: 18 months in French oak; 30% new
Skin Contact: 14 days
Type of Wine: Red
Alcohol: 14,0%
Optimal Serving Temperature: 60 ˚F
Vintage Year: 2016
Bottle Format: 750ml

deVilliers

Varietals: Pinot Noir (100%)
Barrel Aging: 18 months in French oak; 30% new
Skin Contact: 14 days
Type of Wine: Red
Alcohol: 14,0%
Optimal Serving Temperature: 60 ˚F
Vintage Year: 2016
Bottle Format: 750ml

Ryan

Varietals: Pinot Noir (100%)
Barrel Aging: 18 months in French oak; 30% new
Skin Contact: 14 days
Type of Wine: Red
Alcohol: 14,0%
Optimal Serving Temperature: 60 ˚F
Vintage Year: 2016
Bottle Format: 750ml

Mt. Harlan Chardonnay

Varietals: Chardonnay (100%)
Barrel Aging: 15 months in French oak; 30% new
Type of Wine: White
Alcohol: 14,0%
Optimal Serving Temperature: 58 ˚F
Vintage Year: 2016
Bottle Format: 750ml

Central Coast Chardonnay

Varietals: Chardonnay (100%)
Barrel Aging: 10 months in French oak; 10% new
Type of Wine: White
Alcohol: 14,0%
Optimal Serving Temperature: 58 ˚F
Vintage Year: 2016
Bottle Format: 750ml

CORNERSTONE CELLARS

Napa, CALIFORNIA

www.cornerstonecellars.com
E-mail: info@cornerstonecellars.com
Address: 1465 1st Street, Napa, CA
94559 | 850 Bordeaux Way Suite 6,
Napa, CA 94558
Phone: (707) 945-0388

HISTORY

Since 1991 Cornerstone Cellars has been on a quest to deliver on the potential of the Napa Valley's finest mountain and benchland Cabernet Sauvignon vineyards. Since that time, their signature winemaking style of firm structure and nuanced texture have attracted an ever-growing number of Cornerstone Cellars admirers, while remaining true to Napa's robust, delicious wine profile on the world wine stage. Signature Varietals include Howell Mountain Cabernet Sauvignon, Benchlands Napa Valley Cabernet Sauvignon and Napa Valley Sauvignon Blanc.

OWNERSHIP & MANAGEMENT

Michael Dragutsky established Cornerstone Cellars in 1991. Twenty-eight years in, the next generation of Cornerstone Cellars sales and winemaking teams bring to market a diverse portfolio of Cabernet Sauvignon wines –of which each one delivers a focused flavor profile - with realistic pricing to match.

WINEMAKER

Winemaker, Charles Thomas has been a dynamic force in winemaking in Napa Valley for over 30 years. Driven by his involvement and passion for great vineyards, his relentless pursuit of excellence has fostered innovative viticultural and winemaking practices. Charles was responsible for the Robert Mondavi Reserve and Napa Valley wines from the 1980's to

1994. The first twelve vintages of Opus One were produced under his care. He redefined Kendall-Jackson's Cardinale, and launched Lokoya and Verite. For five years, he produced exceptional wines at Rudd Oakville and Edge Hill. Most recently, he directed the modernization of the vineyards at Quintessa, creating wines of unprecedented quality from the estate.

Winemaker, Kari Auringer has contributed to the fame of some of the Napa Valley's most luminous names including Scarecrow, Lindstrom, Keever, Kelly Fleming and Corra and has been singled out as a rising star in Napa Valley winemaking. Kari believes her success is a combination of dedication, hard work, talent and working with great people. Kari describes herself as a hands-on winemaker and gladly immerses herself in all aspects of the winemaking process from vineyard to bottle.

VINEYARD
They carefully source grapes from the best vineyards each year. These vineyards have a variety of different soil types.

109 TONNES

GRAPES SOURCED
- Cabernet Sauvignon
- Pinot Noir
- Sauvignon Blanc
- Cabernet Franc
- Merlot

Cornerstone wines are available via their website, their two tasting rooms and are distributed to several states around the country.

Top restaurants that serve Cornerstone Wines

1. Bistro Jeanty, Yountville, CA
2. Chez Philippe at The Peabody Hotel, Memphis, TN
3. Booth One, Chicago, IL
4. Hotel Via, San Francisco, CA
5. Dream Hotel, Nashville, TN
6. The Ritz Carlton, Atlanta, GA
7. The Q Restaurant, Napa, CA
8. Rutherford Grill, Rutherford, CA

VISITOR INFORMATION
The winery and tasting rooms can be visited with appointment only. Tastings are available at a cost.

WINES

Calistoga Cabernet Sauvignon

Varietals: Cabernet Sauvignon (95%), Merlot (5%)
Barrel Aging: 18 months in French oak; 75% new
Type of Wine: Red
Alcohol: 14,9%
Vintage Year: 2015
Bottle Format: 750ml

Howell Mountain Cabernet Sauvignon

Varietals: Cabernet Sauvignon (95%), Merlot (5%)
Barrel Aging: 18 months in French oak; 70% new
Type of Wine: Red
Alcohol: 14,5%
Vintage Year: 2015
Bottle Format: 750ml

Benchlands Cabernet Sauvignon

Varietals: Cabernet Sauvignon (86%), Petit Verdot (10%), Merlot (4%)
Barrel Aging: 18 months in French oak; 80% new
Type of Wine: Red
Alcohol: 14,9%
Vintage Year: 2015
Bottle Format: 750ml

Atlas Peak Cabernet Sauvignon

Varietals: Cabernet Sauvignon (100%)
Barrel Aging: 18 months in French oak; 70% new
Type of Wine: Red
Alcohol: 15,5%
Vintage Year: 2014
Bottle Format: 750ml

Somona Valley Sauvignon Blanc

Varietals: Sauvignon Blanc (100%)
Barrel Aging: 10 months in 45% concrete, 22% acacia, 22% stainless Steel, 11% French oak
Type of Wine: White
Alcohol: 14,1%
Vintage Year: 2017
Bottle Format: 750ml

Rutherford Benchlands Cabernet Sauvignon

Varietals: Cabernet Sauvignon (100%)
Barrel Aging: 18 months in French oak; 80% new
Type of Wine: Red
Alcohol: 14,9%
Vintage Year: 2015
Bottle Format: 750ml

FOPPIANO VINEYARDS

Healdsburg, CALIFORNIA

www.foppiano.com
E-mail: info@foppiano.com
Address: 12707 Old Redwood Highway, Healdsburg CA
Phone: (707) 433-7272

HISTORY
Founded in 1896 by Giovanni Foppiano, Foppiano Vineyards is one of Sonoma County's oldest continually-operated, family-owned wineries. The family has supplied Northern California with wine for over a century, surviving Prohibition in the 1920s by selling home winemaking kits. They believe that through the strength of the family and a commitment to quality, their traditions can be maintained and can thrive. They are proud to be one of the founding members of the Russian River Valley AVA, and continue to enjoy the fruits of their hardworking Italian heritage. To stay on the cutting edge of quality winemaking, they have made important investments in infrastructure and winery equipment throughout the years. The vision of the fifth generation of Foppianos, together with Giovanni's foresight to purchase land in the Russian River Valley, guides the family into the future while creating a world class wine program representative of their history.

OWNERSHIP & MANAGEMENT
The winery and vineyards are owned 100% by the Foppiano Family. The Board is composed of family members representing the 4th and 5th generations. Paul Foppiano, is the President and Vineyard Manager. Rob McNeill is the Vice President and General Manager. Other key management personel include, Heidi Neumainville, Finance Manager, Kirsti Harley, Director of Marketing and Public Relations, Nova Perrill, Winemaker and Andreanna DeForest, Tasting Room Manager.

WINEMAKER
Winemaker, Nova Perrill, joined Foppiano Vineyards in the beginning of 2015 and embodies the essence of what Foppiano represents: a commitment to quality in the cellar and vineyard. He brings with him not only the knowledge and experience gained from over 10 years of winemaking in Sonoma County, but also a strong desire to continue to enrich and expand the legacy of Foppiano Vineyards. Often times likening wine to art, he recognizes the subjectivity of wine and strives to create a masterpiece that many, from those just starting to explore wine to the ultimate wine enthusiast, can enjoy. After having already earned his Bachelor of Science degree from California State University, San Luis Obispo, Nova had decided to go back for his Master's degree in Crop Science when he found himself drawn to winemaking. At first attracted by the farming aspect, he quickly found himself intrigued by how, like art, this hands-on process could create such an enjoyable end result.

This winning combination of education, inquisitiveness, and respect landed him in the role of Assistant Winemaker and Viticulturist at Mount Eden Vineyards where he worked with

small batches of award winning Pinot Noir and Chardonnay for four years. Nova soon recognized that to become a well-rounded winemaker he needed to learn more about what winemaking and production involved beyond the realm of boutique winemaking. So in 2008 he moved on to become the Assistant Winemaker at Dry Creek Vineyards where he mastered making quality wine that was more widely available. Within his 7 years there he not only expanded his repertoire but also learned to quickly and accurately recognize which technique could make a wine truly shine.

Nova brings to Foppiano Vineyards a very simple philosophy: to maintain the quality of the wine from grape to glass by letting the fruit guide the way. He does this by making sure he "stays in touch with the cellar" and employs the hands-on technique that attracted him to this industry in the first place. It enables him to really get a feel for what is happening to the wine throughout every step of the winemaking process. When speaking of the future of the Foppiano line-up of wines, Nova cites not only the quality of the fruit that comes from the vineyards, but also the successful legacy of the winery and family.

VINEYARD

The winery owns 131 acres of land, out of which 119 acres are under vine. The majority of the land consists of the soil type, pleasantan gravelly loam, a well-drained soil ideal for winegrapes. Vineyard blocks closest to the river have a larger percentage of gravel and sand in the soil mix. Vineyard blocks to the East of the winery are similar and related though they contain a percentage of clay as part of the makeup.

GRAPES GROWN

- Petite Sirah
- Pinot Noir
- Sauvignon Blanc
- Chardonnay
- Zinfandel
- Cabernet Sauvignon
- Carignane
- Barbara
- Vermentino

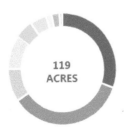

119
ACRES

328
TONNES

In their fermentation process, they employ a varity of fermentation regimens to produce their wine. Vessels vary from oak barrels, small open-top stainless steel tanks, to enclosed stainless steel tanks. Different approaches to fermentation management are employed to capture the qualities of each variety from each unique vintage. This can include choice of yeast, fermentation temperature, pre-fermentation cold-soaking, punch-down and pump-over regimes, and post-fermentation maceration.

Foppiano wines are available at the winery and are distributed throughout the country. They are also exported to Sweden, Canada, Taiwan and China.

Top restaurants that serve Foppiano Wines

1. Hearthstone, Breckenridge, CO
2. Uncommon Ground, Chicago, IL
3. The Harvest, Montauk, NY
4. Bell, Book and Candle, New York, NY
5. Blue Plate Oysterette, Santa Monica, CA
6. Cucina Pardiso, Petaluma, CA
7. Trattoria Contadina Restaurant, San Francisco, CA
8. Portside Tavern, Hyannis, NH
9. Gather Restaurant, Berkeley, CA
10. Mendocino Hotel, Mendocino, CA

VISITOR INFORMATION
The winery and tasting rooms can be visited without appointment. Tastings are available at a cost. They receive approximately 5,500 visitors annually. The winery is also available for private events.

WINES

Della's Block Chardonnay

Varietals: Chardonnay (100%)
Barrel Aging: 14 months in French oak; 75% new
Type of Wine: White
Alcohol: 14,5%
Optimal Serving Temperature: 55-60° F
Vintage Year: 2016
Bottle Format: 750ml
Awards: Gold Medal, Sunset Magazine

Estate Pinot Noir

Varietals: Pinot Noir (100%)
Barrel Aging: 18 months in French oak; 73% new
Type of Wine: Red
Alcohol: 14,5%
Optimal Serving Temperature: 63° F
Vintage Year: 2016
Bottle Format: 750ml
Awards: Gold Medal, 2018 Sonoma County
Harvest Fair

Estate Petite Sirah

Varietals: Petite Sirah (100%)
Barrel Aging: 22 Months in French, Hungarian
and American oak
Type of Wine: Red
Alcohol: 14,9%
Vintage Year: 2014
Bottle Format: 750ml
Awards: Gold Medal, Houston Rodeo Wine
Competition

Estate Sauvignon Blanc

Varietals: Sauvignon Blanc (24%)
Barrel Aging: Stainless steel
Type of Wine: White
Alcohol: 14,2%
Optimal Serving Temperature: 50-55° F
Vintage Year: 2017
Bottle Format: 750ml
Awards: Triple Gold Medal, Best of Class, 2018
Dan Berger International Wine Challenge

Grant Station Carignane

Varietals: Carignane (100%)
Barrel Aging: 14 months in French and
Hungarian oak
Type of Wine: Red
Alcohol: 14,0%
Vintage Year: 2016
Bottle Format: 750ml
Awards: Gold Medal, 2018 Orange County Wine
Society Challenge

Estate Chardonnay

Varietals: Chardonnay (100%)
Barrel Aging: 8 months in French oak; 30% new
Type of Wine: White
Alcohol: 14,3%
Vintage Year: 2017
Bottle Format: 750ml
Awards: Silver Medal, 2018 Sonoma County
Harvest Fair; Gold Medal, Houston Rodeo Wine
Competition

Estate Zinfandel

Varietals: Zinfandel (100%)
Barrel Aging: 18 months in 30% new French and
70% Hungarian oak
Type of Wine: Red
Alcohol: 14,9%
Optimal Serving Temperature: 63° F
Vintage Year: 2015
Bottle Format: 750ml
Awards: Gold Medal, Orange County Wine
Society

Nonno's Block Zinfandel

Varietals: Zinfandel (100%)
Barrel Aging: 20 months in 50% new French
and 50% Hungarian oak
Type of Wine: Red
Alcohol: 14,9%
Optimal Serving Temperature: 63° F
Vintage Year: 2016
Bottle Format: 750ml
Awards: Double Gold Medal, 2018 Sonoma
County Harvest Fair

Gianna's Block Petite Sirah

Varietals: Petite Sirah (100%)
Barrel Aging: 28 months in French oak; 60% new
Type of Wine: Red
Alcohol: 14,9%
Optimal Serving Temperature: 63° F
Vintage Year: 2015
Bottle Format: 750ml
Awards: Double Gold Medal, 2018 Sonoma
County Harvest Fair

SKINNER VINEYARDS & WINERY

Somerset, CALIFORNIA

www.skinnervineyards.com
E-mail: info@skinnervineyards.com
Address: 8054 Fairplay Road, Somerset, CA 95684
Phone: (530) 620-2220

HISTORY

In 2006 Mike and Carey Skinner resurrected their family's wine-making legacy by re-establishing Skinner Vineyards & Winery in the Sierra Foothills. Mike's great-great-great grandfather, James Skinner, was a Scottish miner who established and ran the original Skinner winery from 1861 through the early 1900's. When Mike first learned about James Skinner's history and his suddenly rich Gold Rush heritage, he was so excited he couldn't sleep. "I'm the first son of the first son of the first son of the first son of the first son," he said. Carey was just as caught up in the embrace of both family history and adventure, and her husband's enthusiasm became her enthusiasm too.

Mike and Carey are committed to making elegant Rhône-style wines that express the distinct qualities of our granitic soils and meticulously farmed, high elevation vineyards. With the new Skinner Vineyards, they hope to weave their history with the bright future of the foothills and unite their love of family, nature, food and wine.

OWNERSHIP & MANAGEMENT

Both Mike and Carey Skinner were successful business people who were happy in their careers, Carey with years in Southern California real estate and Mike running his own insurance company in Los Angeles. Both were very active in their community including coaching kids and mentoring, and both had long histories exploring food and wine. But this was different. "This," Carey says, "was passion. It's the way we both want to live our lives."

Only months after learning about the Skinner legacy, they bought land around the old

Skinners township, unreservedly embraced their newfound heritage, and began creating Skinner Vineyards & Winery. Today, neither has an official winery title beyond founders, because, as Carey says, "everyone does everything that's needed." Mike focuses on winery operations, Carey on sales and marketing, but it depends on the day.

WINEMAKER

Director of Winemaking, Adam Smith, raised in El Dorado County, has cut a wide swath in winemaking in his journey back to the foothills. He honed his craft in the Willamette Valley in Oregon at Domaine Serene, Bethel Heights Vineyards and Shea Wine Cellars. He then ventured beyond Oregon to New Zealand's Craggy Range before being lured to the Sonoma Coast as Winemaker for Banshee Wines. Then the Willamette Valley called him back, where his return saw, first, the collaboration with Jean-Nicolas Méo of Domaine Méo Camuzet in Burgundy to establish Domaine Nicolas-Jay and most recently, reconnecting with Banshee Wines to establish their Oregon brand, Averaen Wines.

VINEYARD

The winery owns 150 acres of land, out of which 35 acres are under vine. The White Oak Flats with an elevation of 1,310 feet is composed of iron rich volcanic clay loam with quartz and granite scattered throughout. The Stoney Creek Vineyard with an elevation of 2,700 feet is situated on a saddleback ridgeline with steep slopes and various aspects. Soils are comprised of corse decomposed granite. The newest vineyard site, Wing Ranch, is situated between 1,350 and 1,400 feet in elevation with east and northeast facing hillside aspects, and is comprised of sandy clay loam soils.

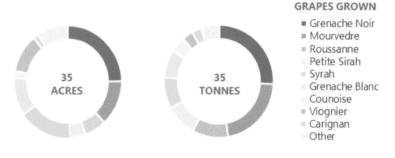

GRAPES GROWN

- Grenache Noir
- Mourvedre
- Roussanne
- Petite Sirah
- Syrah
- Grenache Blanc
- Counoise
- Viognier
- Carignan
- Other

35 ACRES

35 TONNES

VISITOR INFORMATION

The winery and tasting rooms can be visited without appointment. Tours and tastings are available at a cost. Group tours are also available. They receive over 8,000 visitors annually.

WINES

Grenache Blanc

Varietals: Grenache Blanc (100%)
Barrel Aging: 6 months in 65% French oak and 35% stainless steel
Type of Wine: White
Alcohol: 13,6%
Vintage Year: 2017
Bottle Format: 750ml

Mourvèdre

Varietals: Mourvèdre (99%), Grenache (1%)
Barrel Aging: 11 months in French oak
Type of Wine: Red
Alcohol: 13,6%
Vintage Year: 2016
Bottle Format: 750ml

Estate Mourvèdre

Varietals: Mourvèdre (100%)
Barrel Aging: 18 months in French oak; 6% new
Type of Wine: Red
Alcohol: 14,2%
Vintage Year: 2015
Bottle Format: 750ml

Eighteen Sixty-One

Varietals: Grenache Noir (54%), Mourvèdre (34%), Syrah (12%)
Barrel Aging: 18 months in French oak
Type of Wine: Red
Alcohol: 14,6%
Vintage Year: 2015
Bottle Format: 750ml

Grenache Noir

Varietals: Grenache Noir (100%)
Barrel Aging: 11 months in French oak
Type of Wine: Red
Alcohol: 14,5%
Vintage Year: 2016
Bottle Format: 750ml

Syrah

Varietals: Syrah (88%), Grenache (10%), Viognier (2%)
Barrel Aging: 23 months in French oak; 24% new
Type of Wine: Red
Alcohol: 14,6%
Vintage Year: 2015
Bottle Format: 750ml

Petite Sirah

Varietals: Petite Sirah (100%)
Barrel Aging: 23 months in French oak; 13% new
Type of Wine: Red
Alcohol: 15,2%
Vintage Year: 2015
Bottle Format: 750ml

WENTE VINEYARDS

Livermore, CALIFORNIA

www.wentevineyards.com
E-mail: concierge@wentevineyards.com
Address: 5565 Tesla Road, Livermore, CA 94550
Phone: (925) 456-2305

HISTORY

Founded in 1883, Wente Family Estates is the oldest continuously-operated family-owned winery in the country, owned and managed by the 4th and 5th generations of the Wente family. The family owns estate vineyards in the Livermore Valley, San Francisco Bay and Arroyo Seco, Monterey appellations. All of their wines are distributed throughout the United States and select brands are featured in over 75 countries worldwide. In 2010, Wente Family Estates was among the first wineries to receive the Certified California Sustainable Vineyard and Winery designation, and one of the only wineries to certify every aspect of its business. In 2011, Wente Family Estates was named American Winery of the Year by Wine Enthusiast and a top 30 wine company by Wine Business Monthly. With the deepest respect for the knowledge passed down from previous generations, the 4th and 5th generations of the Wente family continue their vision for wine quality and integrity through passion, dedication and pursuit of excellence.

OWNERSHIP & MANAGEMENT

Wente Vineyards is owned and operated by the 4th and 5th generation Wente family members. Eric Wente, 4th generation winegrower is the Chairman of the Board. Philip Wente, 4th generation winegrower is the co-founder of Murrieta's Well. Carolyn Wente, 4th generation winegrower serves as the CEO, and Karl Wente, 5th generation winegrower, serves as both Chief Operating Officer and Chief Winemaker. Other members of the family from the 5th generation are Christine Wente, President of Wente Foundation for Arts Education, Niki Wente, Viticulturist and Jordan Wente, Project Manager.

VINEYARD

Wente Vineyards has 3,000 acres are under vine. The soil type is different at each vineyard.

At Wente, they use both native yeasts and a selection of cultured yeasts. The diversity of yeasts that they use in the winemaking process helps to illuminate the diversity of their vineyards. The complexity brought by using a multitude of different fermentations with their own yeast profiles to craft the final blend allows the winemakers to best showcase each of Wente's beautiful wines.

They use a variety of different fermentation strategies at Wente. They ferment in: concrete, stainless steel, open-top, French oak, American oak and neutral oak barrels. On occasion they will ferment multiple varieties together to create a wine that is more complex than either of it's individual parts.

VINES PLANTED

- Chardonnay
- Cabernet Sauvignon
- Petite Sirah
- Petit Verdot
- Merlot
- Riesling
- Pinot Noir
- Sauvignon Blanc
- Zinfandel
- Cabernet Franc

3,000 ACRES

Wente wines are available throughout their property (tasting rooms, golf course and restaurant), across the country in restaurants, bars and retail shops. The wines are also exported to over 75 countries.

Top restaurants that serve Wente Wines

1. PF Changs, various locations
2. Morton's Steakhouse, various locations
3. Brio & Bravo Restaurants,various locations
4. Tadich Grill, San Francisco, CA
5. Hilton Hotels, various locations worldwide
6. Stiltsville Fish Bar, Miami Beach, FL
7. J Alexanders, various locations
8. Mizuna, Denver, CO
9. Rosebud, Chicago, IL
10. Glass & Vine, Miami Beach, FL

VISITOR INFORMATION

The winery and tasting rooms can be visited without appointment. Tours and tastings are available at a cost. Group tours (maximum 30 people) are also available. The winery receives about 45,000 visitors annually and is also available for private events.

WINES

Riva Ranch Vineyard Chardonnay

Varietals: Chardonnay (98%), Gewürztraminer (2%)
Barrel Aging: 8 months in French oak; 60% new
Type of Wine: White
Alcohol: 13,5%
Optimal Serving Temperature: 50 ˚F
Vintage Year: 2017
Bottle Format: 750ml
Awards: Double Gold Medal, 2017 San Francisco International Wine Competition; Gold Medal, 2017 Los Angeles International Wine Competition

Morning Fog Chardonnay

Varietals: Chardonnay (98%), Gewürztraminer (2%)
Barrel Aging: Stainless steel
Type of Wine: White
Alcohol: 13,5%
Optimal Serving Temperature: 50 ˚F
Vintage Year: 2017
Bottle Format: 750ml
Awards: Gold Medal, 2018 San Antonio Stock Show & Rodeo Wine Competition

Wetmore Vineyard Cabernet Sauvignon

Varietals: Cabernet Sauvignon (79%), Petite Sirah (9%), Petit Verdot (8%), Malbec (4%)
Barrel Aging: 18 months in French oak; 40% new
Type of Wine: Red
Alcohol: 14,5%
Optimal Serving Temperature: 60-65 ˚F
Vintage Year: 2016
Bottle Format: 750ml
Awards: Gold Medal, 2018 Korea Wine Challenge; Gold Medal, San Diego International Wine Challenge

n^{th} Degree Cabernet Sauvignon

Varietals: Cabernet Sauvignon (90%), Petit Verdot (8%), Malbec (2%)
Barrel Aging: 22 months in French oak; 80% new
Type of Wine: Red
Alcohol: 14,7%
Optimal Serving Temperature: 60-65 ˚F
Vintage Year: 2016
Bottle Format: 750ml

WILSON OF DRY CREEK

Healdsburg, CALIFORNIA

www.wilsonwinery.com
E-mail: info@wilsonwinery.com
Address: 1960 Dry Creek Road,
Healdsburg, CA 95448
Phone: (707) 433-4355

HISTORY

Wilson Winery is distinguished not only by its outstanding wines, but by the twin pillars of family and tradition upon which its reputation rests. The tradition predates the winery's founding in 1993 and is evident in the century-old tin barn that houses the Wilson Winery facility. One of the oldest structures in the legendary Dry Creek Valley, the barn has been lovingly restored by Ken and Diane Wilson to provide a state-of-the-art venue for their award-winning wines, while offering glimpses of both a storied past and a promising future.

Today, modern stainless steel tanks stand in place of the redwood vats that once held the valley's most sought-after wines, and French and American oak barrels line the walls of the historic building. What hasn't changed is the sense of pride that permeates the place, and the focus of quality that finds its way into every bottle. The old tin barn is more than the home of Wilson Winery; it is a landmark that represents the history and tradition of winemaking excellence in the heart of the Dry Creek Valley.

OWNERSHIP & MANAGEMENT

Working out of her Dry Creek location since 1993, Diane Wilson has established herself as a standout winemaker in Sonoma County. She started her winemaking career by winning Best of Class at the Sonoma County Harvest Fair for her wine, unusual for someone without formal winemaking training. The instant success she experienced with her first vintage has continued for more than twenty years. As the creative force behind Wilson Winery and Matrix Winery, Diane continues to accrue a staggering amount of awards each year, recently winning 38 gold and double gold medals for her wines at the Sonoma County Harvest Fair. She uses self-described, unorthodox methods to craft standout wines. Although she learned the basic elements of wine chemistry as a Biochemistry major in college, she says her degree isn't what makes her a great winemaker. Instead, she credits her hands-on, learning along with relying on her senses during the production process to know when it's time to blend or bottle.

This approach has served her well. At the prestigious Sonoma County Harvest Fair, Diane was awarded Sweepstakes Red Wine winner, twice for her Sawyer Zinfandel, once for her Tori Zinfandel, and once for her Matrix Estate Pinot Noir. She was also awarded Sweepstakes Red Wine winner at the San Francisco Chronicle Competition for her Molly's Petite Sirah. At the International Women's Winemaking Competition in 2018, she won three Best of Class awards, as well as Best of Show, earning her the title of International Woman Winemaker of the Year for the third time. In 2018, Diane was awarded her second grand prize from the Houston Rodeo Uncorked International Wine Competition.

Although primarily known as a winemaker, Diane and her husband, Ken Wilson, made their entry in the Dry Creek Valley as grape growers, planting their first vineyards high in the mountains of the northern part of the Dry Creek Valley appellation.

Their love of family is reflected in the naming of their vineyards. Their first holdings were named after their children: Sydney, Victoria and Sawyer Wilson, as well as their parents: Carl, Dorothy, and Ellie. Today, some 25 years later, each of the children has a role in growing the business as well.

VINEYARD
The winery owns 14,000 acres of land, out of which 800 acres are under vine. With most of their Estate Vineyards located in Dry Creek Valley the Wilsons have four of the more common soil types exhibited in their vineyards: yolo loam, manzanita loam, boomer loam and zamora silty clay loam.

Wilson of Dry Creek wines are available via their website and the tasting room.

VISITOR INFORMATION
The winery and tasting room can be visited without appointment. Tours and tastings are available at a cost. Group tours (maximum 15 people) are also available.

WINES

Ellie's Petite Sirah

Varietals: Petit Sirah (92%), Zinfandel (8%)
Barrel Aging: 16 months in French oak
Type of Wine: Red
Alcohol: 15,9%
Vintage Year: 2017
Bottle Format: 750ml

Sydney Petite Sirah

Varietals: Petit Sirah (92%), Zinfandel (8%)
Barrel Aging: 16 months in French oak
Type of Wine: Red
Alcohol: 15,7%
Vintage Year: 2017
Bottle Format: 750ml

Dorothy' Syrah

Varietals: Syrah (100%)
Barrel Aging: 18 months in French oak
Type of Wine: Red
Alcohol: 15,3%
Vintage Year: 2016
Bottle Format: 750ml

Carl's Zinfandel

Varietals: Zinfandel (95%), Petit Sirah (5%)
Barrel Aging: 16 months in French oak
Type of Wine: Red
Alcohol: 15,6%
Vintage Year: 2017
Bottle Format: 750ml

Sawyer Zinfandel

Varietals: Zinfandel (94%), Petit Sirah (6%)
Barrel Aging: 16 months in French oak
Type of Wine: Red
Alcohol: 16,0%
Vintage Year: 2017
Bottle Format: 750ml

Ellie's Old Vine Zinfandel

Varietals: Zinfandel (90%), Petit Sirah (10%)
Barrel Aging: 16 months in French oak
Type of Wine: Red
Alcohol: 15,9%
Vintage Year: 2017
Bottle Format: 750ml

Sydney Zinfandel

Varietals: Zinfandel (95%), Petit Sirah (5%)
Barrel Aging: 16 months in French oak
Type of Wine: Red
Alcohol: 16,0%
Vintage Year: 2017
Bottle Format: 750ml

Molly's Zinfandel

Varietals: Zinfandel (85%), Petit Sirah (15%)
Barrel Aging: 16 months in French oak
Type of Wine: Red
Alcohol: 15,8%
Vintage Year: 2017
Bottle Format: 750ml

Nolan Zinfandel

Varietals: Zinfandel (94%), Petit Sirah (6%)
Barrel Aging: 16 months in French oak
Type of Wine: Red
Alcohol: 15,9%
Vintage Year: 2017
Bottle Format: 750ml

Tori Zinfandel

Varietals: Zinfandel (95%), Petit Sirah (5%)
Barrel Aging: 16 months in French oak
Type of Wine: Red
Alcohol: 16,0%
Vintage Year: 2017
Bottle Format: 750ml

COLORADO CELLARS WINERY

Palisade, COLORADO

www.coloradocellars.com
E-mail: info@coloradocellars.com
Address: 3553 E Road, Palisade, CO 81526
Phone: (970) 464-7921

HISTORY

Modern day Colorado winemaking began in 1974 when Colorado State University – with a grant from the U.S. government – planted test plots of wine grapes throughout the 'four corners' area of the southwest. One of those test plots is located directly in front of the present day winery, and is the oldest commercial Colorado vineyard in existence today. The Colorado Limited Winery Act was enacted in 1977, creating Colorado Limited Winery Licenses, which required the use of Colorado grapes to make wine. Colorado Cellars Winery was founded soon after that in 1978 and, although other entities had bonded as "wineries" prior to that date, Colorado Cellars was the first to produce and sell Colorado wines made from Colorado grapes. Those wines were originally sold under the Colorado Mountain Vineyards brand with the Colorado Cellars brand appearing in 1986 and the Rocky Mountain Vineyards and Orchard Mesa Wine Company brands appearing in 1990.

Owners Richard and Padte Turley assisted with the creation of the Grand Valley American Viticulture Area in 1991 and the Colorado Wine Industry Development Board around the same time. By 1990, there were five Colorado wineries but Colorado Cellars Winery pioneered the production of virtually all the types of Colorado wines made today.

Colorado Cellars currently has a fermentation and storage capacity of over 29,000 gallons, with annual production fluctuating around 12,000 cases, representing over 30 types of wines and dozens of wine-based food items. The original winery building remains nestled underground in a hillside overlooking the Bookcliff Mountains with the Colorado River and Grand Valley stretching out below.

OWNERSHIP & MANAGEMENT

Colorado Cellars is a family owned and operated winery. They grow their own grapes and fruit, keep bees for honey wine, personally make and bottle the wines. They are unique amongst Colorado wineries in that they are and have always been exclusively in the wine business. Richard and Padte Turley, along with their sons, Kyle and Cory, continue to operate the winery on a daily basis.

WINEMAKER

Padte Turley is a pioneer in her field as Colorado's first female winemaker and she oversees virtually every aspect of the winemaking process at Colorado Cellars Winery. She also personally directs and participates in all grape-growing activities on the estate-grown vineyards. Her hands-on approach allows her to closely monitor all the annual variations of the vineyards due to temperature and rainfall, factors which directly affect the quality and quantity of the grape crop and ultimately the unique, premium character of their wines vintage after vintage.

VINEYARD

The winery owns 93 acres of land, of which 33 acres are planted as orchards and vineyards. The vineyard locations were selected as the optimal locations in the valley by the top scientists and researchers of the time. They are some of the original Colorado State University Four Corners Project plantings, whose purpose was to reintroduce wine grape plantings to Colorado's West Slope area. These vineyards are perched high atop the Grand Valley of the Colorado River at 4,800 feet above sea level, and are situated on an ancestral river pediment. Their soils are derived from the shale and sandstone that has been eroded from the uplifted canyons that both surround and shelter the Grand Valley Appellation, creating a unique high altitude microclimate which imparts intense flavor and fruit components to the wines. These enhanced fruit characteristics result in long-lived wines.

The family has always practiced earth friendly farming techniques, which enables them to utilize the natural yeasts occurring in the vineyard. This practice results in subtle flavor nuances in their wines which are supplemented by the addition of selected cultured yeasts which finish the fermentation process.

GRAPES GROWN

- Cabernet Sauvignon
- Syrah
- Pinot Grigio
- Pinot Noir
- Merlot

13 ACRES

70 TONNES

The family's belief that Colorado wines can stand in the company of the great wines of the world has driven them to continue innovations in Colorado grape growing and winemaking. They practice natural growing techniques in their vineyards and orchards such as leaf removal, cluster thinning, cane reduction and canopy management, re-introduction of grape pomace as fertilizer, minimal natural pest control, measured drip irrigation application and gentle hand harvesting. Their winemaking techniques are innovative as well; including extensive cold fermentation with native yeasts, natural fining and filtration and exclusive use of stainless steel fermentation tanks. Selected fermentation occurs in concrete amphora tanks and 600-gallon French oak casks or a mixture of American, French, and Hungarian oak barrels. Their overall philosophy emphasizes minimal processing at all stages. These pioneering methods create their style of Colorado wines – richly flavored, highly complex yet fruit forward –reflecting their high-altitude origins.

Colorado Cellars Winery wines are available at their tasting room and retail liquor and wine shops throughout the state of Colorado. They also ship directly to customers in over 40 states.

VISITOR INFORMATION
The winery and tasting room can be visited without appointment year round. Tours and tastings are available at a minimal cost. Group tours (maximum 50 people) are also available. The winery receives about 40,000 visitors annually and their landscaped grounds are available for private events.

WINES

Alpenglo Riesling

Varietals: Riesling (100%)
Type of Wine: White
Alcohol: 12,0%
Optimal Serving Temperature: 45° F
Vintage Year: 2017
Bottle Format: 750ml

Cabernet Sauvignon

Varietals: Cabernet Sauvignon (100%)
Barrel Aging: 12 months in new French oak
Skin Contact: 1 month
Type of Wine: Red
Alcohol: 13,0%
Optimal Serving Temperature: 65° F
Vintage Year: 2016
Bottle Format: 750ml

Colorado Mountain Vineyards

Varietals: Field blend
Barrel Aging: 9 months in French oak
Skin Contact: 1 month
Type of Wine: Red
Alcohol: 13,0%
Optimal Serving Temperature: 65° F
Vintage Year: 2016
Bottle Format: 750ml

Pinot Grigio

Varietals: Pinot Grigio (100%)
Type of Wine: White
Alcohol: 12,0%
Optimal Serving Temperature: 45° F
Vintage Year: 2017
Bottle Format: 750ml

Trinity Champagne

Varietals: Pinot Noir (100%)
Barrel Aging: 2 months
Type of Wine: Sparkling
Alcohol: 12,0%
Optimal Serving Temperature: 45° F
Vintage Year: 2018
Bottle Format: 750ml

Port Wine

Varietals: Field blend
Barrel Aging: 3 months in French oak
Skin Contact: 1 month
Type of Wine: Fortified
Alcohol: 18,0%
Optimal Serving Temperature: 65° F
Vintage Year: 2018
Bottle Format: 500ml

DAMIANI WINE CELLARS

Burdett, NEW YORK

www.damianiwinecellars.com
E-mail: info@damianiwinecellars.com
Address: 4704 State Route 414,
Burdett, NY 14818
Phone: (607) 546-5557

HISTORY

Founders of Damiani Wine Cellars Lou Damiani and Phil Davis both grew up in Hector. Lou had a long time interest in winemaking and originally went to school for food science before switching into engineering. In the mid nineties he returned to studying winemaking in a serious way and mentored under other winemakers for a number of years. In 1996 Lou wanted to plant his first vineyard of Cabernet Franc and Merlot and went to his old friend and collegemate Phil Davis who was a long time viticulturist. The two of them threw themselves into the project and the following year Phil pulled out his own hybrid vineyard and planted Cabernet Sauvignon, Pinot Noir and Merlot. The two friends and partners soon started making some world class red wines. They officially became Damiani Wine Cellars in 2004. The journey has never slowed down and they have included many varieties of grapes and types of wine, always striving for excellence and expression of the unique terroir of the Finger Lakes region.

In 2007 they hired Glenn Allen as Business Consultant. After working together over the course of the following year Lou and Phil asked Glenn to join them as partner. Since then, Damiani Wine Cellars has expanded both the winery operations and the properties that it now owns and operates. Today, Damiani Wine Cellars has four main vineyard sites and a new tasting room that hosts an event space as well as their retail outlet.

OWNERSHIP & MANAGEMENT

Damiani Wine Cellars is owned and operated by three friends, Lou Damiani, Phil Davis and Glenn Allen. Lou was the Head Winemaker from inception in 2003 until 2011 when he helped to train Phil Arras to continue and improve the tradition at Damiani Wine Cellars. As original winemaker, Lou established the winery's reputation for bold full bodied reds and

elegant whites. If asked, he humbly will give credit to grower Phil Davis, who is responsible for attaining the most complex expression of flavors possible from each vineyard. With an eye for setting the highest standards, Glenn has helped lead them into the vanguard of small wineries changing the landscape for the Finger Lakes AVA.

WINEMAKER

Phil Arras grew up in Philadelphia and moved to the finger lakes in 2003 to attend Cornell University, where he studied philosophy and political science. After taking a class on wine appreciation, he was bit by the wine bug and resolved to go back to school for winemaking, but before he could make it to California he was hired by Damiani Wine Cellars in 2009 as Assistant Winemaker and decided to try out learning on the job. After several years, Phil became the Head Winemaker in 2012. He also runs a small mobile wine bottling company, providing bottling services for several small local wineries.

VINEYARD

The winery owns 24 acres of land, and leases another 10 acres, all of which is under vine. They have several vineyards nestled along the east side of Seneca lake. The Finger Lakes were carved out by the last glacial period which left behind dramatic landscapes and a complex matrix of soil types. Each vineyard has is own terroir which is influenced by the closeness to the lake, slope, aspect to the sun and soil composition. In general, all soils are

GRAPES GROWN

- Cabernet Sauvignon
- Pinot Noir
- Cabernet Franc
- Merlot
- Pinot Grigio
- Lemberger
- Gewürztraminer
- Chardonnay
- Sauvignon Blanc
- Pinot Munier

34
ACRES

94
TONNES

deep gravelly loam on shale bedrock, with a moderate slope and close proximity to the lake. They are gravelly loamy glaciofluvial deposits containing significant amounts of limestone. Their vineyards are located on the south east side of Seneca Lake, which is affectionately known as "The Banana Belt" since this area receives more sunlight and heat than anywhere else in the Finger Lakes.

Their red wine philosophy is to age in barrels to impart just enough oak to gently frame the fruit, rather than to deliver a big oak profile. They want the beautiful flavors of the fruit to come through. As a cool climate region, their fruit tends to be delicate, nuanced and crisp, offering lip-smacking lively wines. For most of their red wines, they tend to use older neutral barrels and age for 8 months. For their Reserve red wines, which are only made in the very best vintages, they use newer oak barrels and age for 12 to 24 months.

Most of their whites are steel-tank fermented under careful temperature control. The Rieslings are made from several small tanks, where they use a separate treatment with yeast and whole-berry versus crushed fruit, which gives them multiple layers from which to build the finished wine. The Gewürztraminer undergoes extended cold soak maceration and is slow-fermented in neutral oak barrels over several months. This preserves the intense aromatics while giving an unusually broad pallet and full mouthfeel.

Damiani Wine Cellars wines are available at their tasting room, via their website and are distributed throughout the state of New York.

Top restaurants that serve Damiani Wine Cellars Wines

1. Purdy's Farmer and Fish, North Salem, NY
2. Boulevard Seafood Company, New York, NY
3. Latourelle Resort & Spa, Ithaca, NY
4. Lento, Rochester, NY
5. Hudson Farmer & The Fish, Sleepy Hollow, NY
6. Justines, Cobleskill, NY
7. Brown Hound Downtown, Rochester, NY
8. Hazelnut Restaurant, Trumansburg, NY
9. Red Dove Tavern, Geneva, NY
10. 677 Prime, Albany, NY

VISITOR INFORMATION
The winery and tasting room can be visited without appointment. Tastings and tours are available at a cost. Group tours (maximum 15 people) are also available. The winery receives about 5,000 visitors annually and is also available for private events.

WINES

Meritage

Varietals: Cabernet Sauvignon (55%), Merlot (27%), Cabernet Franc (18%)
Barrel aging: 15 months in American oak; 15% new
Type of Wine: Red
Alcohol: 13,8%
Optimal Serving Temperature: 63° F
Vintage Year: 2016
Bottle Format: 750ml

MC²

Varietals: Merlot (38%), Cabernet Franc (33%), Cabernet Sauvignon (29%)
Barrel aging: 8 months in French oak
Type of Wine: Red
Alcohol: 13,0%
Optimal Serving Temperature: 63° F
Vintage Year: 2017
Bottle Format: 750ml

Cabernet Franc

Varietals: Cabernet Franc (100%)
Barrel aging: 9 months in French oak
Type of Wine: Red
Alcohol: 13,7%
Optimal Serving Temperature: 63° F
Vintage Year: 2017
Bottle Format: 750ml

Lemberger

Varietals: Lemberger(100%)
Barrel aging: 8 months in neutral oak
Type of Wine: Red
Alcohol: 12,5%
Optimal Serving Temperature: 63° F
Vintage Year: 2017
Bottle Format: 750ml

Pinot Noir

Varietals: Pinot Noir (100%)
Barrel aging: 18 months in neutral oak
Type of Wine: Red
Alcohol: 13,5%
Optimal Serving Temperature: 63° F
Vintage Year: 2014
Bottle Format: 750ml

Riesling

Varietals: Riesling (100%)
Barrel aging: 7 months in stainless steel
Type of Wine: White
Alcohol: 12,0%
Optimal Serving Temperature: 55° F
Vintage Year: 2017
Bottle Format: 750ml

Dry Rosé

Varietals: Pinot Noir (100%)
Barrel aging: 6 months in stainless steel
Type of Wine: Rosé
Alcohol: 12,0%
Optimal Serving Temperature: 50° F
Vintage Year: 2017
Bottle Format: 750ml

Gewürztraminer

Varietals: Gewürztraminer (100%)
Barrel aging: 8 months in French oak
Type of Wine: White
Alcohol: 13,7%
Optimal Serving Temperature: 55° F
Vintage Year: 2017
Bottle Format: 750ml

Chardonnay

Varietals: Chardonnay (100%)
Barrel aging: 6 months in French oak
Type of Wine: White
Alcohol: 13,7%
Optimal Serving Temperature: 55° F
Vintage Year: 2016
Bottle Format: 750ml

Bollicine

Barrel aging: Cayuga (72%), Pinot Noir (17%), Chardonnay (10%), Pinot Munier (1%)
Barrel aging: Stainless steel
Type of Wine: Sparkling
Alcohol: 11,0%
Optimal Serving Temperature: 40° F
Bottle Format: 750ml

BILLSBORO WINERY

Geneva, NEW YORK

www.billsborowinery.com
E-mail: kim@billsborowinery.com
Address: 4760 State Route 14, Geneva NY 14456
Phone: (315) 789-9538

HISTORY

Billsboro Winery is a winemaker-owned winery, committed to crafting dry, classic European varietal wines, grown by Seneca Lake's best vineyards. Owned by Kim and Vincent Aliperti, the winery is dedicated to small-scale production, allowing them to devote more attention to providing a high quality product.

OWNERSHIP & MANAGEMENT

A lot of people fall in love with the idea of becoming a winemaker, and a honeymoon is probably one of the most typical moments to have such fantasies. But most of the people don't then come home and become successful winemakers. That's the story of Vincent Aliperti, winemaker and owner of Billsboro Winery. He's been making wine now for over 20 years. Together with his wife Kim, a long-time wine enthusiast and manager of operations, the two own and operate Billsboro Winery. Their dynamic approach has earned praise both locally and nationally.

Starting out in the Hamptons of Long Island, he apprenticed for three vintages between 1997 and 1999 at Wolffer Estate under long-time winemaker Roman Roth, producing mostly Chardonnay and Merlot. In early 2000, Vincent moved his family to the Finger Lakes to work at the legendary Hermann J. Wiemer Vineyard, where he was first exposed to Riesling production. In 2001 Vincent joined then startup Atwater Estate Vineyards, where he continues today heading up winemaking operations of over 15 different varieties. Vincent's winemaking style is often described as crisp and fruit-driven with a focus on creating intense but balanced wines.

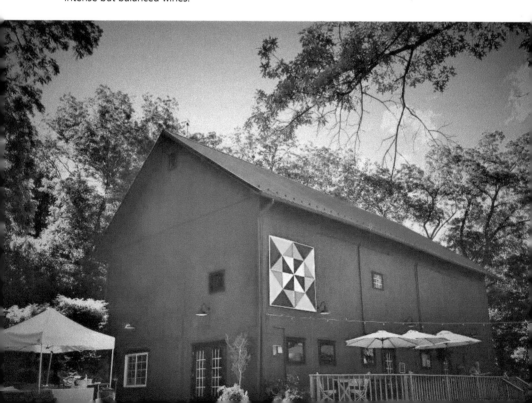

VINEYARD

The winery sources its grapes from Sawmill Creek Vineyards. Sawmill Creek Vineyards in Hector, New York is located along the southeast corner of Seneca Lake. Its steep-sided, southwest facing vineyards are widely recognized as among the best in the Finger Lakes.

Billsboro wines are available at many of the region's best local restaurants as well as select New York City and Brooklyn eateries. The wines are also distirbuted to Philadelphia and Boston.

VISITOR INFORMATION

The winery and tasting room can be visited without appointment. Tastings are available at a cost. The winery receives about 11,000 visitors annually and is also available for private events.

WINES

Cabernet Sauvignon

Varietals: Cabernet Sauvignon (100%)
Type of Wine: Red
Alcohol: 13,9%
Vintage Year: 2016
Bottle Format: 750ml

Syrah

Varietals: Syrah (98%), Cabernet Sauvignon (2%)
Type of Wine: Red
Alcohol: 13,8%
Vintage Year: 2016
Bottle Format: 750ml

Chardonnay

Varietals: Chardonnay (100%)
Type of Wine: White
Alcohol: 13,2%
Vintage Year: 2016
Bottle Format: 750ml

Dry Riesling

Varietals: Riesling (100%)
Type of Wine: White
Alcohol: 12,2%
Vintage Year: 2016
Bottle Format: 750ml

Sauvignon Blanc

Varietals: Sauvignon Blanc (100%)
Type of Wine: Red
Alcohol: 12,8%
Vintage Year: 2017
Bottle Format: 750ml

Sawmill Creek Vineyards Pinot Noir

Varietals: Pinot Noir (100%)
Type of Wine: Red
Alcohol: 13,9%
Vintage Year: 2016
Bottle Format: 750ml

Cabernet Franc

Varietals: Cabernet Franc (100%)
Type of Wine: Red
Alcohol: 13,9%
Vintage Year: 2017
Bottle Format: 750ml

Albarino

Varietals: Albarino (100%)
Type of Wine: White
Alcohol: 12,9%
Vintage Year: 2017
Bottle Format: 750ml

Pinot Gris

Varietals: Pinot Gris (100%)
Type of Wine: White
Alcohol: 12,6%
Vintage Year: 2017
Bottle Format: 750ml

Après

Varietals: Vignoles (100%)
Type of Wine: Sweet
Alcohol: 11,5%
Vintage Year: 2017
Bottle Format: 375ml

DR. KONSTANTIN FRANK WINERY

Hammondsport, NEW YORK

www.drfrankwines.com
E-mail: info@drfrankwines.com
Address: 9749 Middle Road,
Hammondsport, NY 14840
Phone: (800) 320-0735

HISTORY

Dr. Konstantin Frank ignited the "Vinifera Revolution" a movement that forever changed the course of wine growing in the Finger Lakes. Dr. Frank's vision, knowledge and determination are credited with elevating the New York wine industry from a state of happy mediocrity to a level that today commands world attention. A European immigrant, Dr. Frank and his family arrived in the United States in 1951. After a brief stay in New York City, Dr. Frank, a professor of Plant Sciences who held a Ph.D. in Viticulture, moved upstate to take a position at Cornell University's Geneva Experiment Station.

Dr. Frank believed from his years in the Ukraine that the lack of proper rootstock, not the cold climate, was the reason for the failure of Vitis Vinifera vines in the Finger Lakes region. He continued to promote his beliefs and to seek a sympathetic ear, which he found in Charles Fournier, a French champagne maker and President of nearby Gold Seal Vineyards. Communicating in French, Dr. Frank revealed his research for growing the delicate European vinifera grape varieties in cold climates. For the first time the Northeastern United States could produce European varieties of wines.

In 1962, merely a decade after arriving in America, Dr. Frank founded the winery, which quickly earned a reputation for spectacular Rieslings, and its original planting of vines formed the backbone of New York's world-class wines and champagnes.

OWNERSHIP & MANAGEMENT

The winery is currently run by 3rd and 4th generation, Fred Frank and Meaghan Frank. Willy's son, Frederick Frank, took over leadership of the winery in 1993. Fred's business degree

from Cornell University and his study of Viticulture and Enology in Germany helped prepare him to take over the family business. Under Fred's leadership the winery's production and amount of medals earned has increased greatly and he looks forward to one day turning over the reins to his daughter, Meaghan Frank. Meaghan received her MBA degree from the University of Adelaide in Australia, which has one of the top wine business programs in the world. In addition, Meaghan has completed her second Master's degree in Enology from Cornell University in 2015. With combined expertise in wine business and winemaking, Meaghan plans to revolutionize the winery experience as well as the quality of the wines.

WINEMAKER
Head Winemaker, Mark Veraguth, a native to Santa Rosa, California, joined Dr. Konstantin Frank Winery in 1989 as Assistant to Head Winemaker, Barbara Frank. In his youth, Mark studied at the University of California, Davis earning his Bachelor's of Science degree in Civil Engineering. During his studies, Mark was working as a cellar and vineyard helper at S. Anderson Vineyards. He found that his skills in production and logistics of civil engineering translated well to the wine industry and decided to never leave. Mark became Head Winemaker of Dr. Konstantin Frank Winery in 2004 and is currently on his 29th vintage.

VINEYARD
The winery owns 247 acres of land, out of which 126 acres are under vine. They have two different vineyard areas on Keuka Lake and Seneca Lake. Their original vineyard is located on Keuka Lake with many varieties planted in the 1950's and 1960's. The soils are generally shallow, slate based with high natural acidity. The vineyards are east facing with slopes leading to Keuka Lake. The proximity to the deepest part of Keuka Lake moderates the temperatures throughout the year. Their Seneca Lake vineyards were planted in 2007. The west facing vineyards are located in the warmest microclimate in the Finger Lakes due to their proximity to the deepest parts of Seneca Lake. The soils are deep honeoye silt loam.

They have a selection of yeasts that they use depending on grape variety and vintage conditions. They sometimes use multiple yeasts in different tanks to add complexity during the blending stage. In general, their white grapes are direct-pressed without skin contact.

Red grapes generally always receive a few days of cold soak before crushing. Majority of their white grapes are fermented in temperature controlled stainless steel tanks at cooler temperatures to preserve varietal character. Some of their Chardonnay is barrel fermented. They produce a skin-contact style of Rkatsiteli where the skins are in contact with the juice throughout fermentation. Their red grapes are generally fermented in open-top stainless steel vats with manual punch-downs three times per day during fermentation.

GRAPES GROWN
- Riesling
- Pinot Noir
- Rkatsiteli
- Chardonnay
- Gruner Veltliner
- Pinot Grigio
- Gewurztraminer
- Blaufrankisch
- Cabernet Sauvignon
- Other

126 ACRES

Dr. Konstantin Frank wines are available in almost 40 states in the United States, and are also exported to Aruba, Canada, Dominican Republic, Japan, New Zealand, Singapore and United Kingdom.

Top restaurants that serve Dr. Konstantin Frank Wines

1. Café Boulud, New York, NY
2. David Burke Kitchen, New York, NY
3. Gramercy Tavern, New York, NY
4. Morimoto, New York, NY
5. Rainbow Room, New York, NY
6. The Smith, New York, NY
7. Auberge de Soleil, Napa Valley, CA
8. Tavern on the Green, New York, NY
9. Prezza, Boston, MA
10. Vernick, Philadelphia, PA

VISITOR INFORMATION
The winery and tasting room can be visited without appointment. Tours and tastings are available at a cost. Group tours (maximum 10 people) are also available. They receive 60,000 visitors annually.

WINES

Dry Riesling

Varietals: Riesling (100%)
Type of Wine: White
Alcohol: 12,5%
Optimal Serving Temperature: 47 ˚F
Vintage Year: 2017
Bottle Format: 750ml

Blanc de Noirs

Varietals: Pinot Noir (95%), Pinot Meunier (5%)
Skin Contact: 24 hours
Type of Wine: Sparkling
Alcohol: 12,5%
Optimal Serving Temperature: 44 ˚F
Vintage Year: 2013
Bottle Format: 750ml

Eugenia Dry Riesling Single Vineyard

Varietals: Riesling (100%)
Type of Wine: White
Alcohol: 12,9%
Optimal Serving Temperature: 47 ˚F
Vintage Year: 2017
Bottle Format: 750ml

Blanc de Blancs

Varietals: Chardonnay (100%)
Type of Wine: Sparkling
Alcohol: 12,1%
Optimal Serving Temperature: 44 ˚F
Vintage Year: 2013
Bottle Format: 750ml

Grüner Veltliner

Varietals: Grüner Veltliner (100%)
Type of Wine: White
Alcohol: 12,0%
Optimal Serving Temperature: 47 ˚F
Vintage Year: 2017
Bottle Format: 750ml

Old Vines Pinot Noir

Varietals: Pinot Noir (100%)
Barrel Aging: 18 months in French oak
Skin Contact: 3 days
Type of Wine: Red
Alcohol: 13,0%
Optimal Serving Temperature: 58 ˚F
Vintage Year: 2016
Bottle Format: 750ml

Rkatsiteli

Varietals: Rkatsiteli (100%)
Type of Wine: White
Alcohol: 12,0%
Optimal Serving Temperature: 47 ˚F
Vintage Year: 2017
Bottle Format: 750ml

Hilda Chardonnay Single Vineyard

Varietals: Chardonnay (100%)
Barrel Aging: 9 months in French oak; 50% new
Type of Wine: White
Alcohol: 13,3%
Optimal Serving Temperature: 50 ˚F
Vintage Year: 2017
Bottle Format: 750ml

FULKERSON WINERY

Dundee, NEW YORK

www.fulkersonwinery.com
E-mail: contact@fulkersonwinery.com
Address: 5576 State Route 14, Dundee, NY 14837
Phone: (607) 243-7883

HISTORY

In 1805, Caleb Fulkerson journeyed north from a settlement in New Jersey in search of fertile farmland. He staked out a piece of land on the western slopes of Seneca Lake. Caleb's son Samuel inherited the farm in 1840 and built the farmhouse that stands on the property today. Samuel died at the age of 43, leaving behind his wife Jane and seven young children. Jane never remarried, but she held the farm and kept her six sons out of the Civil War. Harlan Paye Fulkerson Sr. was the only son to stay on the farm, which he bought from his brothers and sister. He took care of his mother and had one son with his wife Phoebe. The farm's main crop was black raspberries. Under the direction of Harlan Paye Fulkerson Jr., black raspberries became the first significant commercial crop for the farm.

Grapes had been grown on the farm since the 1830s, but it wasn't until a blight wiped out the raspberry industry in the 1960s that Roger Fulkerson began expanding grape plantings. Sayre Fulkerson graduated from Cornell University in 1975 with a degree in Pomology and now serves as Fulkerson's Winemaker. Sayre and his wife Nancy opened Fulkerson Winery in 1989. They also continued to expand the farm's grape juice production, attracting a loyal and growing following of home winemakers.

OWNERSHIP & MANAGEMENT

Sayre Fulkerson started to produce wine on a commercial level in 1989. With expansions in 1993, 1997, 2004, and again in 2015, the business now employs 15 full-time personnel and up to 50 throughout the year.

Steven Fulkerson represents the 7th generation of Fulkersons to work this land. He graduated from Cornell University in 2007 with a degree in Viticulture and Enology and has been General Manager since 2015. Steven and his wife Regina are proud parents to the 8th generation, Sarah Fulkerson, born October 2018.

VINEYARD

The winery owns 350 acres of land, and leases another 2 acres, out of which 112 acres are under vine. The vineyards have a mix of alluvial soils from an ancient river delta mainly consisting of Howard Gravel, Odessa Clay, Dunkirk and Langford.

In their fermentation process, they use commercially available yeast strains that are developed for clean fermentations and varietal specific character. Their fermentation style can be summarized in a "fruit first" mentality. They have a unique style called "juicy sweet" that resembles a Auslese style. Grapes are fermented to optimum sweetness without the addition of any sugar.

GRAPES GROWN

- Riesling
- Concord
- Cayuga
- Diamond
- Niagara
- Noiret
- Vincent
- Ravat 51
- Vidal
- Other

112 ACRES

380 TONNES

Fulkerson wines are available in New York, Florida and Luxembourg.

Top restaurants that serve Fulkerson Wines

1. Watkins Glen Harbor Hotel, Watkins Glen, NY
2. Beer Tree Brewing Company, Binghamton, NY
3. French Louie, Brooklyn, NY
4. Buttermilk Channel, Brooklyn, NY
5. Julia's Beer and Wine Bar, Ridgewood, NY
6. No. 7, Brooklyn, NY
7. Casa Antica, Lewiston, NY
8. Vineyard at Winham, Windham, NY
9. Justines, Cobleskill, NY
10. 1000 Islands Harbor Hotel, Clayton, NY

VISITOR INFORMATION
The winery and tasting room can be visited without appointment. Tours and tastings are available at a cost. Group tours (maximum 20 people) are available. The winery receives about 35,000 visitors annually and is also available for private events.

WINES

Syrah

Varietals: Syrah (100%)
Barrel Aging: 8 months in stainless steel
Skin Contact: 2 weeks
Type of Wine: Red
Alcohol: 12,0%
Optimal Serving Temperature: 65° F
Vintage Year: 2017
Bottle Format: 750ml
Awards: Gold Medal, Dan Berger International Wine Competition

Red Blend

Varietals: Cabernet Franc (50%), Noiret (50%)
Barrel Aging: 24 months in French oak
Skin Contact: 2 weeks
Type of Wine: Red
Alcohol: 12,0%
Optimal Serving Temperature: 65° F
Bottle Format: 750ml

Albarino

Varietals: Albarino (100%)
Type of Wine: White
Alcohol: 12,0%
Optimal Serving Temperature: 50° F
Vintage Year: 2017
Bottle Format: 750ml

Dry Riesling

Varietals: Riesling (100%)
Type of Wine: White
Alcohol: 12,0%
Optimal Serving Temperature: 50° F
Vintage Year: 2017
Bottle Format: 750ml

Bourbon Barrel Aged Syrah

Varietals: Syrah (100%)
Barrel Aging: 3 months in new bourbon
Skin Contact: 2 weeks
Type of Wine: Red
Alcohol: 12,0%
Optimal Serving Temperature: 65° F
Vintage Year: 2016
Bottle Format: 750ml

Sauvignon Blanc

Varietals: Sauvignon Blanc (100%)
Skin Contact: 5 hours
Type of Wine: White
Alcohol: 12,0%
Optimal Serving Temperature: 50° F
Vintage Year: 2017
Bottle Format: 750ml

Grüner Veltliner

Varietals: Grüner Veltliner (100%)
Type of Wine: White
Alcohol: 12,0%
Optimal Serving Temperature: 50° F
Vintage Year: 2017
Bottle Format: 750ml

Matinee

Varietals: Himrod (100%)
Type of Wine: Sweet White
Alcohol: 10,0%
Optimal Serving Temperature: 50° F
Bottle Format: 750ml

Fulkerson Winery Photos by Steven Fulkerson, Stu Gallagher and Heather Goodreau

PAUMANOK VINEYARDS

Aquebogue, NEW YORK

www.paumanok.com
E-mail: info@paumanok.com
Address: 1074 Main Road, PO Box 741, Aquebogue, NY 11931
Phone: (631) 722-8800

HISTORY
Established in 1983, Paumanok is an estate winery located on the North Fork of Long Island owned and operated by the Massoud Family. From its inception, Paumanok's focus has been to grow the highest quality wines. Paumanok's guiding philosophy is that only the healthiest, ripest grapes will produce great wine - there is no substitute. Paumanok produces several varietal and blended wines with fruit originating from its 86 acres of vineyards. Paumanok produces New York's only Chenin Blanc along with Chardonnay, Riesling, Sauvignon Blanc, Cabernet Franc, Cabernet Sauvignon, Merlot, Petit Verdot, and Pinot Noir.

Paumanok has been recognized with numerous accolades over the years including wine service at The White House, NY Wine & Food Classic's "Winery of the Year" Award, "outstanding" reviews in Robert Parker's Wine Advocate and a nomination for Wine Enthusiast's "American Winery of the Year".

OWNERSHIP & MANAGEMENT
Today, Paumanok is one of a handful of Long Island wineries that is still owned and operated by the founders, making it one of Long Island's oldest and most established wineries. Founders Charles and Ursula are still active ensuring that their three sons continue to manage Paumanok on the same path of quality that they have pursued from the beginning, and to set the stage for the third generation to continue in that endeavor. The three sons are all involved: Kareem is Winemaker, Nabeel is Vineyard Manager and Salim is Administrative Manager.

Born in Bahrain in 1972, Kareem was living with his parents, Charles and Ursula, in Connecticut when they decided to search for real estate to plant a vineyard. In 1983, they founded Paumanok Vineyards in Aquebogue, New York, on the North Fork of Long Island. After earning a Bachelor's of Science degree in Economics from the Wharton School at the University of Pennsylvania, Kareem had a brief career in New York City as a private equity analyst at a private investment firm. He decided to move on and he returned to his family's estate winery.

Kareem has been actively involved with his family's wine making business since its inception, and he has been working full time at Paumanok since 1998. Kareem is a second

generation winemaker, having learned the trade under his father's tutelage. His international travels to South Africa, France, New Zealand and Chile have given him a wide range of experience in the art of wine making.

VINEYARD
The winery own 126 acres of land, out of which 86 acres are under vine. The topography on the North Fork is primarily flat. However, they succeed as a winegrowing region because the soils drain incredibly well. The top soils are a sandy loam followed by sandy gravelly subsoils below enabling excellent drainage. Vineyard Manager Nabeel Massoud has been involved in the family business since its inception. He has been working full time managing the vineyards at Paumanok since 2003. The winegrowing team at Paumanok believes strongly that the wine is made in the vineyard, so Nabeel's role is all important.

For red wines, the grapes are sent through the crusher-destemmer with the rollers set wide apart to retain a larger number of whole berries. Next, the grapes are sorted to remove matter other than grape and any unripe or undesirable fruit. The must is inoculated immediately with yeast and within 24 hours with malolactic bacteria. This co-inoculation results in the completion of malolactic fermentation prior to the completion of alcoholic fermentation. Delestage is done to achieve thorough, gentle extraction while minimizing the extraction of harsher tannins by the elimination of seeds as the cap settles during delestage. This method ensures that only the softest tannins are extracted. After the fermentation is complete, the free run is drained into oak barrels. The must is pressed and, after clarification, is also moved to oak barrels.

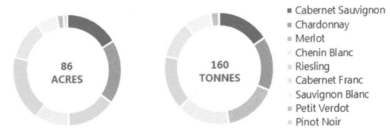

GRAPES GROWN
- Cabernet Sauvignon
- Chardonnay
- Merlot
- Chenin Blanc
- Riesling
- Cabernet Franc
- Sauvignon Blanc
- Petit Verdot
- Pinot Noir

86 ACRES

160 TONNES

For stainless steel fermented white wines, average fermentation temperature is kept cool, around 60° F. The wine is fermented entirely in stainless steel tanks to preserve varietal character. For barrel-aged white wines, the clear juice is inoculated with yeast strain, isolated in Burgundy in barrel fermentation. This is a slow acting yeast, which is what they prefer, in order to preserve as much of the fruitiness as possible. The fermenting must is then transferred to the oak barrels where alcoholic fermentation is completed. Thereafter the wine is inoculated to promote the malolactic fermentation. They want the oak to play asupporting role, integrating well with the fruit rather than featuring it as a recognizable component of the wine.

Paumanok wines are available at their tasting room and at select wine shops and restaurants.

Top restaurants that serve Paumanok Wines

1. ilili, New York, NY
2. Jewel, Melville, NY
3. Gramercy Tavern, New York, NY
4. The Modern, New York, NY
5. North Fork Table and Inn, Southold, NY
6. Almond, New York and Bridgehampton, NY
7. Buddakan, New York, NY
8. The American Hotel, Sag Harbor, NY
9. A lure, Greenport, NY
10. The Halyard, Greenport, NY

VISITOR INFORMATION
The winery and tasting room can be visited without appointment. Tours and tastings are available at a cost. Group tour (maximum 25 people) are also available. The winery receives about 25,000 visitors annually and is available for private events.

WINES

Cabernet Sauvignon – Tuthills Lane Vineyard

Varietals: Cabernet Sauvignon (100%)
Barrel Aging: 17 months in French oak; 33% new
Skin Contact: 14-21 days
Type of Wine: Red
Alcohol: 13,9%
Optimal Serving Temperature: 60° F
Vintage Year: 2014
Bottle Format: 750ml

Petit Verdot - Apollo Drive Vineyard

Varietals: Petit Verdot (100%)
Barrel Aging: 16 months in French oak; 33% new
Skin Contact: 14-21 days
Type of Wine: Red
Alcohol: 13,9%
Optimal Serving Temperature: 60° F
Vintage Year: 2013
Bottle Format: 750ml

Merlot Grand Vintage

Varietals: Merlot (100%)
Barrel Aging: 16 months in French oak; 33% new
Skin Contact: 14-21 days
Type of Wine: Red
Alcohol: 13,0%
Optimal Serving Temperature: 60° F
Vintage Year: 2013
Bottle Format: 750ml

Cabernet Franc Grand Vintage

Varietals: Cabernet Franc (100%)
Barrel Aging: 16 months in French oak
Skin Contact: 14-21 days
Type of Wine: Red
Alcohol: 13,5%
Optimal Serving Temperature: 60° F
Vintage Year: 2014
Bottle Format: 750ml

Blanc de Blancs

Varietals: Chardonnay (100%)
Type of Wine: Sparkling
Alcohol: 12,0%
Optimal Serving Temperature: 40° F
Vintage Year: 2014
Bottle Format: 750ml

Dry Riesling

Varietals: Riesling (100%)
Type of Wine: White
Alcohol: 11,0%
Optimal Serving Temperature: 52° F
Vintage Year: 2017
Bottle Format: 750ml

Chardonnay

Varietals: Chardonnay (100%)
Barrel Aging: 6 months in French oak
Type of Wine: White
Alcohol: 13,0%
Optimal Serving Temperature: 56° F
Vintage Year: 2016
Bottle Format: 750ml

Chenin Blanc

Varietals: Chenin Blanc (100%)
Type of Wine: White
Alcohol: 11,0%
Optimal Serving Temperature: 52° F
Vintage Year: 2018
Bottle Format: 750ml

SHELDRAKE POINT WINERY

Ovid, NEW YORK

www.sheldrakepoint.com
E-mail: finewine@sheldrakepoint.com
Address: 7448 County Road 153
Ovid, NY 14521
Phone: (607) 532-9401

HISTORY
Sheldrake Point Winery is named for the prominent point of land on which it sits, located on the western shore of Cayuga Lake. Operated as an orchard and dairy farm from 1850 to the mid-1980s, the 155-acre lakeshore farm lay fallow until 1997 when a small group of wine enthusiasts organized the purchase of the land and founded the winery. As of 2019, Sheldrake Point Winery continues the agricultural tradition with 55 acres of vineyard planted to 10 vitis vinifera varieties, which are used to make approximately 8,500 cases of estate grown, produced, and bottled wines.

Sheldrake Point Winery was twice named New York State Winery of the Year, and has been listed among the Top 100 Wineries by Wine & Spirits magazine in three different years.

OWNERSHIP & MANAGEMENT
Chuck Tauck and his wife Fran Littin are the owners of Sheldrake Point Winery. Chuck was attracted to the Finger Lakes wine industry during his graduate work at the Cornell Hotel School and was instrumental in the transformation of the old abandoned dairy farm to today's winery and vineyard. As principle owners, he and his wife Fran assume the risk of the venture and personally see to its priorities and requirements. Chuck's focus is on the management and company systems and processes. When not in the office, he and Fran may also be working with the staff, doing repairs, tending the gardens, or chatting with visitors.

WINEMAKER

With experience developed in wineries throughout the Finger Lakes, Winemaker Dave Breeden can always be found in the winery or lab, gently and patiently tending to the fermentation and aging of the wines while caring for the tanks, barrels, and equipment. Armed with two degrees in chemistry and two in philosophy, Dave not only brings expertise in the wine lab and on the crush pad, but he can also be heard waxing poetic on everything from Plato's cave to contemporary third-party politics. 'Inside Dave' joined the Sheldrake Point team in 2002.

VINEYARD

Sheldrake Point's vineyards have been managed since 1999 by Dave Wiemann. The twenty-year teamwork of 'Inside Dave' and 'Outside Dave' has been a key element in the quality of the fruit and the quality of the wine. Wedged between two deep gorges, the east-facing vineyard gently slopes almost to the water's edge, with more than 400-foot depths just off the beach. This positioning creates a unique mesoclimate in which the grapes grow, hindering early bud break in the spring, lowering daily swings in temperature, promoting effective air drainage, lengthening the growing season by more than two weeks, and delaying the onslaught of autumn frosts. The soils at Sheldrake Point are predominantly well-drained, Howard gravelly loam glacially-deposited atop shale, limestone, and slate; considered ideal for grape growing.

GRAPES GROWN

- Cabernet Franc
- Riesling
- Pinot Grigio
- Pinot Noir
- Chardonnay
- Gewürztraminer
- Gamay Noir
- Merlot
- Cabernet Sauvignon
- Other

50 ACRES

226 TONNES

At Sheldrake Point Winery they primarily utilize commercial yeasts while also experimenting with spontaneous fermentations. At Sheldrake Point Winery they embrace the adage that great wine is made in the vineyard, and their winemaking and vineyard teams work closely to ensure that the grapes they pick are of the highest quality and optimal ripeness. Over the years, they have honed their approach to winemaking so that the focus is on terroir. This means that they produce the best wines possible in any given year with as little human intervention as possible, letting the vineyard and vintage truly shine.

Sheldrake Point wines are available at the winery and in New York State with limited distribution along the eastern United States.

Top restaurants that serve Sheldrake Point Wines

1. Ithaca Beer Company, Ithaca, NY
2. The Marshal, New York, NY
3. Argos Inn, Ithaca, NY
4. Aurora Inn, Aurora, NY
5. Dianne & Elisabeth, New York, NY
6. Eddie O'Briens Grille & Bar, Geneva, NY
7. Vanguard, New York, NY
8. Larchmont Yacht Club, Larchmont, NY
9. Corkbuzz Wine Studio, New York, NY
10. Label 7, Pittsford, NY

VISITOR INFORMATION
The winery and tasting room can be visited without appointment. Tastings are available at a cost. Groups of 8 to 20 people are welcomed with advance appointment. The winery receives over 22,000 visitors annually and is also available for small private events.

WINES

Dry Riesling

Varietals: Riesling (100%)
Type of Wine: White
Alcohol: 13,3%
Optimal Serving Temperature: 45° F
Vintage Year: 2016
Bottle Format: 750ml

Gamay Noir

Varietals: Gamay Noir (95%), Syrah (5%)
Barrel Aging: 6 months in French oak
Skin Contact: 11 days
Type of Wine: Red
Alcohol: 12,7%
Optimal Serving Temperature: 50° F
Vintage Year: 2017
Bottle Format: 750ml

Dry Rosé

Varietals: Cabernet Franc (100%)
Skin Contact: 12 hours
Type of Wine: Rosé
Alcohol: 12,0%
Optimal Serving Temperature: 45° F
Vintage Year: 2017
Bottle Format: 750ml

Gewürztraminer

Varietals: Gewürztraminer (100%)
Type of Wine: White
Alcohol: 14,3%
Optimal Serving Temperature: 45° F
Vintage Year: 2016
Bottle Format: 750ml

Riesling Ice Wine

Varietals: Riesling (100%)
Type of Wine: White
Alcohol: 11,8%
Optimal Serving Temperature: 45° F
Vintage Year: 2016
Bottle Format: 375ml

Cabernet Franc

Varietals: Cabernet Franc (100%)
Barrel Aging: 7.5 months in French and American oak
Skin Contact: 14 days
Type of Wine: Red
Alcohol: 12,7%
Optimal Serving Temperature: 55° F
Vintage Year: 2017
Bottle Format: 750ml

Pinot Gris

Varietals: Pinot Gris (100%)
Type of Wine: White
Alcohol: 14,0%
Optimal Serving Temperature: 45° F
Vintage Year: 2016
Bottle Format: 750ml
Awards: Gold Medal, Jefferson Cup Invitational

SILVER THREAD VINEYARD

Lodi, NEW YORK

www.silverthreadwine.com
E-mail: info@silverthreadwine.com
Address: 1401 Caywood Road, Lodi, NY 14860
Phone: (607) 582-6116

HISTORY

Silver Thread's original 6-acre vineyard was established in 1982, and its ecologically-designed wine cellar was built in 1995 by organics enthusiast and wine writer Richard Figiel. Planted on the eastern shore of Seneca Lake on shallow, shale-heavy soils, the vineyard takes great advantage of a distinctly warm microclimate within the otherwise cool Finger Lakes district. Silver Thread has always been known for following the principles of sustainable farming, and even held an organic certification for a period of time in the 1990s. Since the winery's first release in 1991, Silver Thread has earned critical acclaim for its wines, especially Riesling, Chardonnay, Gewurztraminer and Pinot Noir. Since assuming ownership in 2011, new owners Paul Brock and his wife Shannon have expanded the estate vineyard to 8 acres and elevated the quality and consistency of the wines. Silver Thread's commitment to premium, terroir-driven wines attracts a loyal following of wine aficionados to its off-the-beaten path location.

OWNERSHIP & MANAGEMENT

Heralded winemaker Paul Brock and respected wine educator Shannon Brock have owned and operated Silver Thread Vineyard since 2011. Both hold degrees from Cornell University and the Wine & Spirit Education Trust. Paul Brock has crafted a portfolio of intense and high-quality wines that have been immediately well-received by Finger Lakes wine devotees.

Winemaker and Co-owner Paul Brock is an Assistant Professor of Viticulture and Wine Technology at Finger Lakes Community College in Geneva, New York. He coordinates the

Associate in Applied Science degree in Viticulture and Wine Technology there, and advises around 50 students through the degree program. Previously, he worked as a commercial winemaker in both the Finger Lakes and Marlborough, New Zealand. Paul has a Master's of Science degree in Enology and Viticulture from Cornell University and a Bachelor's of Science degree in Chemical Engineering from Rensselaer Polytechnic Institute. He has earned a wine judge certification from the American Wine Society and a level three Advanced Certificate in Wines and Spirits from the Wine and Spirit Education Trust of London. He has judged at several regional, state and national wine competitions. Paul is driven by his desire to learn about and explain classical and cutting edge techniques useful to small-scale winemaking and vineyard operations.

General Manager Shannon Brock, who has been a leader in the hospitality industry in the Finger Lakes for over a decade, has put her expertise to work to create outstanding tasting room and wine club experiences at Silver Thread. Mrs. Brock also serves as an instructor for Wine & Spirit Education Trust and teaches at the New York Wine & Culinary Center in Canandaigua, New York.

VINEYARD
The winery covers 27 acres of land, out of which 8 acres are under vine. The vineyard is planted on a glacially-carved slope overlooking the eastern side of Seneca Lake and presents a west-facing aspect. Afternoon sun reflects off the surface of the lake onto the vines, thereby intensifying the sunlight. The main soil type is honeoye silt-loam, and it varies from 12 to 48 inches deep over shale bedrock. Plantings closer to the lake have shallower soil, and the soil depth increases with distance from the lake shore. The vines' roots are able to penetrate the layers of shale thanks to the freeze-thaw cycle that they experience during the winter months. Shale fragments are found on the surface and throughout the soil layer. Due to the shallow soil, the vigor of their vines is controlled, and yields are lower-than-average for the region.

In their fermentation process, they add cultured yeast strains in order to more closely control their fermentations and prevent off-flavors from masking the characteristics of the vineyard. Along with several strains of saccharomyces cerivisea, they regularly use up to four non-saccharomyces species of yeast that are commercially available.

Their primary goal is to express the fruit of their own estate vineyard and the vineyards of their grower-partners. As they only produce 3,000 cases per year, their fermentation process is very hands-on, artisanal and small-scale. They inoculate with selected yeast strains and species. Multiple fermentation temperatures are used to vary yeast enzyme activity and expression of the vineyard. They use mostly stainless steel fermentation vessels, but neutral oak barrels are also employed.

GRAPES GROWN

- Riesling
- Pinot Noir
- Cabernet Franc
- Gewurztraminer
- Chardonnay
- Merlot
- Cabernet Sauvignon

8 ACRES

20 TONNES

Silver Thread wines are available in New York, New Jersey, Connecticut, Pennsylvania and Massachusetts. They are also available through their tasting room and their website.

Top restaurants that serve Silver Thread Wines

1. The NoMad Hotel, New York, NY
2. Gramercy Tavern, New York, NY
3. Rouge Tomate, New York, NY
4. Home Restaurant, New York, NY
5. Restaurant Good Luck, Rochester, NY
6. Dano's Heuriger, Lodi, NY
7. Stonecat Café, Hector, NY
8. The Restaurant School at Walnut Hill College, Philadelphia, PA
9. Puritan & Co., Cambridge, MA
10. Mercato, Ithaca, NY

VISITOR INFORMATION

The winery and tasting room can be visited without appointment. Best seasons to visit are Summer and Fall. Winery tours and tastings are available at a cost. The winery receives about 6,000 visitors annually.

WINES

Dry Riesling

Varietals: Riesling (100%)
Type of Wine: White
Alcohol: 12,0%
Optimal Serving Temperature: 50° F
Vintage Year: 2014
Bottle Format: 750ml

Semi-Dry Riesling

Varietals: Riesling (100%)
Type of Wine: White
Alcohol: 11,0%
Optimal Serving Temperature: 50° F
Vintage Year: 2014
Bottle Format: 750ml

Good Earth White

Varietals: Vidal Blanc (80%), Riesling (15%), Gewurztraminer (5%)
Type of Wine: White
Alcohol: 13,0%
Optimal Serving Temperature: 50° F
Vintage Year: 2014
Bottle Format: 750ml
Awards: Double Gold Medal, 2015 New York Wine & Food Classic Competition

Pinot Noir

Varietals: Pinot Noir (100%)
Barrel Aging: 9 months in French oak
Skin Contact: 7 days
Type of Wine: Red
Alcohol: 12,5%
Optimal Serving Temperature: 63° F
Vintage Year: 2013
Bottle Format: 750ml

STV Estate Vineyard Riesling

Varietals: Riesling (100%)
Type of Wine: White
Alcohol: 11,5%
Optimal Serving Temperature: 50° F
Vintage Year: 2014
Bottle Format: 750ml

Gewurztraminer

Varietals: Gewurztraminer (100%)
Type of Wine: White
Alcohol: 13,5%
Optimal Serving Temperature: 50° F
Vintage Year: 2014
Bottle Format: 750ml

Doyle Fournier Vineyard Riesling

Varietals: Riesling (100%)
Type of Wine: White
Alcohol: 12,0%
Optimal Serving Temperature: 50° F
Vintage Year: 2014
Bottle Format: 750ml
Awards: Gold Medal, 2015 New York Wine & Food Classic Competition; Gold Medal, 2015 Finger Lakes AVA Riesling Challenge

A BLOOMING HILL WINERY & VINEYARD

Cornelius, OREGON

www.abloominghillvineyard.com
E-mail:
bloominghillvineyards@gmail.com
Address: 5195 SW Hergert Road,
Cornelius OR 97113
Phone: (503) 992-1196

HISTORY

Jim Witte arrived in Oregon from Southern California in 2000 and planted his vineyard on this beautiful piece of land in the Willamette Valley. As the planting was underway, he also built a stable for his quarter horses and thoroughbreds, completing an idyllic picture. Holly came along in 2005 and they married the next year. Jim hand-tends the vines, produces the wines and does all the bottling and labeling on site in a winery built alongside the barn. Holly tends to A Blooming Hill Vineyard's image and marketing and, together, they hold forth in their Tasting Room that opens onto a patio with a view of majestic Mt. Hood and their lower vineyard. Some people say weekends at the Tasting Room are like being at Holly and Jim's *Salon*. Music every weekend from May to September and special events during the year indoors in the big room with the fireplace make this a very desirable and comfortable place to visit. The wines win consistent praise and awards, the highest award being the many repeat visits to the Tasting Room by Wine Club members and visitors. Their Wine Dog, Trouble, fills out the picture by greeting guests at their cars and ushering them down to the Tasting Room.

OWNERSHIP & MANAGEMENT

Jim and Holly met each other many years ago in New York City where Jim ran a television production company and Holly worked as his inept secretary. Jim's career spanned more than three decades in Chicago, New York and Hollywood. He achieved many firsts and

made an indelible impression on everyone with whom he worked. Holly went on to a different career raising money and writing. Their paths separated in the late 1970s and, although they always knew where the other was, they were not brought together romantically until 2005. They consider themselves so lucky to have found each other and to have each found their passion in the work they do together at A Blooming Hill Vineyard & Winery.

WINEMAKER
Jim Witte studied at Chemeketa Viticulture and Enology program in Salem. While he did not enroll in the degree program, he took all of the courses and made to the Dean's list just about every semester. He volunteered at crush with such distinguished winemakers as Jacques Tardi. Jim tries to preserve what the grapes are expressing when they come in from the vineyard, reflecting the weather of that year.

VINEYARD
The winery owns 40 acres of land, out of which 10 acres are under vine. The vineyard is on a southeast-facing slope in the last hills of the Chehalem Mountain range. Each vine in nestled in windblown, volcanic, silty soil anchored to this basalt range with depths of six to twelve feet. This rich soil, known as cornelius klik-klack bordered by kinton and with some laurelwood throughout, produces grapes lavish in the tastes of the earth and bright fruit. The upper and older vineyard, planted in 2002, gives the wines a spiciness. All of the soil produces soft tannins. It requires careful management so each vine is coaxed by hand to produce full and compact clusters. In this unusual microclimate, the 380 feet elevation is protected by higher hills on three sides from any coastal storms or harsh weather changes. The sun warms the grapes throughout the day producing the sugars and flavors into the peak of the afternoon. The grapes are then cooled by the late afternoon and evening ocean breezes that fan down the Columbia River, skirting the coastal range into this, the northern Willamette Valley. This daily cycle is repeated throughout the fall until the grapes are picked at their peak of ripeness.

GRAPES GROWN
- Pinot Noir
- Pinot Gris
- Riesling
- Chardonnay

10
ACRES

27
TONNES

In their fermentation process they cold-soak as long as they can maintain a temperature of less than 60° F and then add yeast to augment the natural fermentation. Once cold-soaking achieves maximum color extraction, fermentation is started to transform the sugars into alcohol. When complete, less than a week later, the juices are moved into oak barrels to begin a secondary fermentation and aging process. They use French, Hungarian and Oregon oak barrels to achieve an understated balance of oak to fruit taste that gives their complex and superb fruit-forward taste. Over the next year, the wine is monitored and naturally fined. The barrels are topped weekly. The Pinot Noir is cold stabilized and left to rest and age.

A Blooming Hill wines are available at the tasting room and via their website.

VISITOR INFORMATION
The winery and tasting room can be visited without appointment. Tours and tastings are available at a cost. The winery receives about 2,500 visitors annually and is also available for private events.

WINES

GEMINI

Varietals: Pinot Noir (100%)
Barrel Aging: 12 months in oak
Skin Contact: 15 days
Type of Wine: Red
Alcohol: 13,4%
Optimal Serving Temperature: 63° F
Vintage Year: 2014
Bottle Format: 750ml
Awards: Silver Medal, Oregon Wine Awards

Pinot Noir

Varietals: Pinot Noir (100%)
Barrel Aging: 12 months in oak
Skin Contact: 15 days
Type of Wine: Red
Alcohol: 12,6%
Optimal Serving Temperature: 63° F
Vintage Year: 2013
Bottle Format: 750ml
Awards: Gold Medal, Oregon Wine Awards;
Gold Medal, Pinot Noir Shootout

Pinot Noir

Varietals: Pinot Noir (100%)
Barrel Aging: 12 months in oak
Skin Contact: 15 days
Type of Wine: Red
Alcohol: 12,7%
Optimal Serving Temperature: 63° F
Vintage Year: 2011
Bottle Format: 750ml
Awards: Double Gold Medal, Oregon Wine
Awards; Gold Medal, Pinot Noir Shootout; Gold
Medal, Northwest Wine Summit

Mingle

Varietals: Pinot Gris (50%), Chardonnay (30%),
Riesling (20%)
Barrel Aging: 7 months in stainless steel
Type of Wine: White
Optimal Serving Temperature: 52° F
Vintage Year: 2017
Bottle Format: 750ml

TROUBLE

Varietals: Pinot Noir (100%)
Barrel Aging: 12 months in oak
Skin Contact: 15 days
Type of Wine: Red
Alcohol: 13,7%
Optimal Serving Temperature: 63° F
Vintage Year: 2014
Bottle Format: 750ml
Awards: Gold Medal, Oregon Wine Awards

Pinot Noir

Varietals: Pinot Noir (100%)
Barrel Aging: 12 months in oak
Skin Contact: 15 days
Type of Wine: Red
Alcohol: 13,7%
Optimal Serving Temperature: 63° F
Vintage Year: 2012
Bottle Format: 750ml
Awards: Silver Medal, Oregon Wine Awards,
Silver Medal; Northwest Food and Wine Summit;
Silver Medal, Pinot Noir Shootout

Pinot Noir in the Port Style

Varietals: Pinot Noir (100%)
Barrel Aging: 4 years in oak
Skin Contact: 15 days
Type of Wine: Red
Alcohol: 17,0%
Optimal Serving Temperature: 63° F
Vintage Year: 2012
Bottle Format: 500ml
Awards: Gold Medal, International Port
Competition

A Blooming Hill Winery & Vineyard Photos by Wendy Mines

BELLE FIORE WINERY, ESTATE AND VINEYARDS

Ashland, OREGON

www.bellefiorewine.com
E-mail: info@bellefiorewine.com
Address: 100 Belle Fiore Lane, Ashland, OR 97520
Phone: (541) 552-4900

HISTORY

The Kerwin family always dreamed of developing a vineyard and winery. In 2000, they located a 55-acre property in Ashland and began to implement the development of Belle Fiore Winery, Estate and Vineyards. The Kerwins planted the vineyards in 2007, cultivating wine grapes from wine growing regions across Mediterranean Europe. From France's Bordeaux region, they grow Cabernet Sauvignon, Cabernet Franc, Malbec, Petit Verdot and Merlot. From the Rhône, they grow Syrah grapes. From Burgundy, their Pinot Noir grapes are celebrated and esteemed. Belle Fiore also grows Sauvignon Blanc and Sauvignon Musque, two classic French white wine grapes.

Just minutes from the exciting Shakespeare Festival in Ashland, Oregon, Belle Fiore Winery provides a magnificent Italian Wine Pavilion and Mediterranean Chateau to enchant customers. Guests of Belle Fiore tasting rooms savor extraordinary wines and classic food pairings, enjoy live music nightly and winemaker paired dinners and stroll amid scenic gardens and vineyards. The winery's motto is, "*Head, Heart and Hands Together. Celebrate the process of thinking and learning. Put love and thoughtfulness into your work. Be creative in your crafts.*" At Belle Fiore Winery, they keep all these alive in the wines they make.

OWNERSHIP & MANAGEMENT

Owner and General Manager, Edward Kerwin graduated in 1979 and was hired out of college by the U.S. National Aeronautics and Space Administration (NASA) in Houston, Texas. After two years at NASA, he returned to studying history, and while working at Princeton University, obtained a Master's of Science degree in History of Science. Ed then

embarked on a career in medicine and attended the University of Colorado Medical School in Denver. Ed's wife, Karen, also has a diverse educational background, having studied languages in Tours, France, Viareggio, Italy, and Salzburg, Austria. She completed her Bacelor's of Science degree in Biochemistry at the University of California, Davis, and later obtained her Master's degree in Genetic Counseling at the University of Colorado. After years of academic studies, the Kerwin family moved to Medford and Jackson County Oregon in 1993. They have four children.

WINEMAKER

Winemaker, Rob Folin started his winery career in the Willamette Valley at Domaine Serene in 2001. By the time he left in 2008, he had moved up the ranks to become Cellarmaster. However, starting in 2002, his family had started planting grapes in the Rogue Valley. By 2009, the Folin family had 25 acres of vines, a winery and a reputation for making high-end Rhône varietals. In May of 2018, Rob took over the position of Winemaker at Belle Fiore. This opportunity has allowed him to work with other varietals like Montepulciano and Teroldego, grapes that are able to thrive in this area, but aren't widely planted yet. Rob's goal is to continue to produce high-end wines that show a sense of place.

VINEYARD

The winery owns 57 acres of land, out of which 30 acres are under vine. Soil composition is a blend of Brader-Debenger loam and Carney clay.

Belle Fiore wines are fermented and aged in their beautiful, technologically advanced tank room admired by winery guests as they stroll on the Pavilion viewing gallery. Belle Fiore's barrel rooms rest submerged beneath the Wine Pavilion, and maintain a steady 56° F year round for optimal, gentle aging.

GRAPES GROWN

30 ACRES

- Pinot Noir
- Cabernet Sauvignon
- Merlot
- Chardonnay
- Teroldego
- Sauvignon Blanc
- Syrah
- Montepulciano
- Tempranillo
- Other

At Belle Fiore, the majority of ferments are inoculated with carefully selected yeast strains to achieve optimal characteristics. Certain varieties like Syrah and Pinot Noir are fermented in open top stainless steel tanks. Bordeaux varieties are typically fermented in closed top stainless steel tanks. Smaller amounts under 3 tons are fermented in small open top tanks or in microbins.

Belle Fiore wines are available at their tasting rooms in Ashland and wine shops and restaurants in Southern Oregon.

VISITOR INFORMATION
The winery and tasting rooms are open daily and can be visited without appointment. Tours and tastings are available at a cost. Group tours (maximum 15 people) are also available. The winery receives over 5,000 visitors annually, and is also available for private events.

WINES

Chardonnay

Varietals: Chardonnay (100%)
Barrel Aging: 7 months in French oak
Type of Wine: White
Alcohol: 14,0%
Optimal Serving Temperature: 58° F
Vintage Year: 2018
Bottle Format: 750ml

Calypso

Varietals: Chardonany (57%), Caprettone (29%), Verdeho (14%)
Barrel Aging: 80% stainless steel, 20% French oak
Type of Wine: White
Alcohol: 14,1%
Optimal Serving Temperature: 58° F
Vintage Year: 2017
Bottle Format: 750ml

Tempranillo

Varietals: Tempranillo (90%), Teroldego (10%)
Barrel aging: 18 months in French oak; 60% new
Skin Contact: 23 days
Type of Wine: Red
Alcohol: 13,5%
Optimal Serving Temperature: 64° F
Vintage Year: 2015
Bottle Format: 750ml

Caprettone

Varietals: Caprettone (100%)
Barrel Aging: Stainless steel
Type of Wine: White
Alcohol: 13,9%
Optimal Serving Temperature: 58° F
Vintage Year: 2018
Bottle Format: 750ml

Montepulciano

Varietals: Montepulciano (100%)
Barrel aging: French and American oak; 60% new
Skin Contact: 19 days
Type of Wine: Red
Alcohol: 14,9%
Optimal Serving Temperature: 64° F
Vintage Year: 2015
Bottle Format: 750ml

Petit Verdot

Varietals: Petit Verdot (100%)
Barrel aging: 26 months in new French oak
Skin Contact: 24 days
Type of Wine: Red
Alcohol: 13,4%
Optimal Serving Temperature: 64° F
Vintage Year: 2015
Bottle Format: 750ml

Belle Fiore Winery Photos by Antal Ullmann, Richard Romagnoli, Christopher Briscoe and April Metternich

BRANDBORG VINEYARD & WINERY

Elkton, OREGON

www.brandborgwine.com
E-mail: info@brandborgwine.com
Address: 345 First Street PO Box 506
Elkton, OR 97436
Phone: (541) 584-2870

HISTORY

Sue and Terry Brandborg relocated to Elkton Oregon in January 2002, having found their dream piece of property, after a two-year search of coastal river valleys in California and Oregon. Terry had been making wine commercially since 1986 working with cool climate varieties from California's Anderson Valley and Santa Maria Valley. Terry and Sue met at a winetasting in Jackson, Wyoming in 1998, and one year later Sue joined him in San Francisco in 1999. They made wine together in California until moving to Oregon in 2002. Both remain very much involved in all of the hands on

work in the vineyards and the winery. They enjoy what they do and create distinctive wines using traditional methods working with grapes from their own estate vineyard and local Elkton vineyards now more than 30 years old. They produce award-winning Pinot Gris, Riesling, Gewürztraminer, Sauvignon Blanc and Grenache, as well as rosé of Pinot Noir and white Pinot Noir.

OWNERSHIP & MANAGEMENT

Terry began making wine at home in 1975 and started a small label in 1986 in his garage in Fairfax, California. In three years the garage was outgrown and winemaking continued in a rented warehouse space in the Bay Area. The driving passion was always to make elegant Pinot Noir and cool-climate aromatic whites.

Terry and Sue began to look for property up and down the coastal river valleys of California's prime cool-climate regions for a site to grow the wines they both loved best, Pinot Noir, Riesling and Gewurztraminer. While visiting wineries in the Umpqua Valley, they learned that these varieties had been grown in Elkton, Oregon since 1972.

In 2002 they packed up and moved to Elkton. The first vineyard block was planted and a winery was built in time for harvest 2002. The accolades and awards started coming in with the first wines produced utilizing great fruit sourced from local Umpqua Valley and Elkton growers. Since those early years when Terry and Sue were the only workers for both the vineyard and winery, the brand has grown to about 10,000 cases. The winemaking philosophy remains unchanged in the quest to make elegant and seductive Pinot Noirs and racy aromatic whites from the very cool climate.

VINEYARD

Terry and Sue own 145 acres of land, out of which 5 acres are under vine. The Ferris Wheel Estate Vineyard sits at 1,000 feet elevation in the true Oregon Coast Range. The geology of the coast range is terranes, sliced off Pacific seabeds uplifted as the Pacific plate dives

under the North American continental shelf. The soils are Bateman, which are marine sediments, very red in color, indicating very old soils with some clay content which is good for water retention. The vineyard is only 25 miles inland from the coast. The property overlooks the main fork of the Umpqua River, which is the largest drainage between the Columbia River, which divides Oregon and Washington, and the Sacramento which flows into San Francisco Bay.

In the fermentation process, they sometimes let grapes ferment spontaneously and they sometimes add commercial yeast. Whites are either whole-cluster pressed or destemmed to the pnuematic press. Pressed juice is settled before being racked to fermenters, barrels or tanks, depending on type. Reds are destemmed only, they are not crushed. Sometimes few stems are added back. Fermentation is in open-top bins with punch-downs done twice a day by hand. They are pressed off at dryness, settled and barreled within a couple of days, retaining some yeast lees. The wine is not racked or sulfured until malolactic fermentation is complete. The wine will spend 18 months in barrel before bottling.

GRAPES GROWN

▪ Pinot Noir

5
ACRES

20
TONNES

Brandborg wines are available in over 30 states throughout the United States.

Top restaurants that serve Brandborg Wines

1. Reeds American Table, St. Louis, MO
2. Remingtons's, Chicago, IL
3. Gogi's, Jacksonville, OR
4. Nishino, Seattle, WA
5. Crosby's Kitchen, Chicago, IL
6. Jack Rabbit, Portland, OR
7. Stir, Dallas, TX
8. Elevation, Banner Elk, NC
9. Gramercy Tavern, New York, NY
10. B & G Oysters, Boston MA

VISITOR INFORMATION
The winery and tasting rooms can be visited without appointment. Tours and tastings are available at a cost. Group tours (maximum 50 people) are also available. The winery receives about 4,000 visitors annually, and is also available for private events.

WINES

Ferris Wheel Estate Pinot Noir

Varietals: Pinot Noir (100%)
Barrel Aging: 18 months in French oak; 20% new
Skin Contact: 14-20 days
Type of Wine: Red
Alcohol: 13,0%
Optimal Serving Temperature: 63˚ F
Vintage Year: 2014
Bottle Format: 750ml
Awards: Platinum Medal, Northwest Wine
Summit

Love Puppets Pinot Noir

Varietals: Pinot Noir (100%)
Barrel Aging: 18 months in French oak; 30% new
Skin Contact: 14-20 days
Type of Wine: Red
Alcohol: 13,6%
Optimal Serving Temperature: 63˚ F
Vintage Year: 2016
Bottle Format: 750ml

BROOKS

Amity, OREGON

www.brookswine.com
E-mail: janie@brookswine.com
Address: 21101 SE Cherry Blossom Lane, Amity, OR 97101
Phone: (503) 435-1278

HISTORY

Brooks is a reflection of the visionary Portland native, Jimi Brooks. His reverence for the land and vines made him a practitioner of biodynamic farming. The great respect for individuality and mastery of blending allowed his wines to achieve layered depth, texture, flavor and balance. While Jimi is no longer with us, his dynamic spirit lives on through his wines, family and friends. With the outpouring of generosity and friendship from the Oregon wine community, Brooks Wines continues to be family-owned and operated and is stronger than ever. In 2014, the winery expanded into a larger home in the Eola-Amity Hills AVA with a welcoming new tasting room featuring sweeping views of four mountains and an incredible tasting experience in the Willamette Valley.

OWNERSHIP & MANAGEMENT

Pascal Brooks inherited the winery at the age of 8 when his father, Jimi Brooks, passed away suddenly. Jimi's sister, Janie Brooks Heuck has managed the winery since Jimi's death in 2004. In the spring of 2005, Janie hired winemaker Chris Williams, who worked alongside Jimi at WillaKenzie and Maysara wineries.

WINEMAKER

Chris Williams met Jimi Brooks by happenstance, when he sold Jimi some motorcycle parts for an old Moto Guzzi. They became fast friends, and Chris began working at the winery, first for wine club events, then in the cellar. He worked alongside Jimi at WillaKenzie Estate, then later at Maysara Winery. When Jimi passed away unexpectedly on the eve of the 2004 harvest, Chris was one of the friends and winemakers who jumped in to help Brooks carry

on and was hired full-time in 2005. He has brought continuity to Brooks wines, sharing Jimi's philosophy and style, and continuously showcases the elegance of small-production Riesling and Pinot Noir from the Willamette Valley.

VINEYARD

The winery owns 20 acres of land, and leases another 10 acres, out of which 29 acres are under vine. Brooks' estate vineyard is east-facing at an elevation of 450 to 750 feet and is largely composed of volcanic, basalt and sedimentary soils. The vineyard is dry-farmed, and has been farmed biodynamically since 2002. They obtained Demeter certification in 2012. Depending on the vintage, their production is 2.5 to 3.5 tons per acre.

They ferment all reds spontaneously. The estate whites are also fermented naturally, and the remaining whites are inoculated. Grapes are hand-picked and sorted during the pick. No SO_2 is added after pressing. Pinot Noir is cold-soaked for 7 to 10 days. All wines are fermented in small 250-gallon tanks at the lowest possible temperatures. No nutrients are added. For cold stability, they use the ambient outside temperature; for heat stability, they use bentonite. Wines are never racked. They gently filter via cross-flow and sterile filter.

GRAPES GROWN

- Pinot Noir
- Riesling
- Pinot Grigio
- Muscat
- Pinot Meunier

29
ACRES

67
TONNES

Brooks wines are available at the tasting room and at restaurants and retailers throughout the United States, Canada, Japan, and the UK.

Top restaurants that serve Brooks Wines

1. Alinea, Chicago, IL
2. Gramercy Tavern, New York City, NY
3. Slanted Door, San Francisco, CA
4. Landmarc, New York City, NY
5. Republique, Los Angeles, CA
6. Blackbird, Chicago, IL
7. McCrady's, Charleston, SC
8. Wild Ginger, Seattle, WA
9. Barcelona, Boston, MA
10. R'Evolution, New Orleans, LA

VISITOR INFORMATION

The winery and tasting rooms can be visited without appointment. Tastings and tours are available at a cost. Group tours (maximum 12 people) are also available. The winery receives about 32,000 visitors annually and is also available for private events.

WINES

Janus

Varietals: Pinot Noir (100%)
Barrel Aging: 18 months in oak; 80% new
Skin Contact: 10-14 day
Type of Wine: Red
Alcohol: 13,2%
Optimal Serving Temperature: 63° F
Vintage Year: 2012
Bottle Format: 750ml

Runaway

Varietals: Pinot Noir (100%)
Barrel Aging: 10 months in French oak
Skin Contact: 10-14 day
Type of Wine: Red
Alcohol: 13,5%
Optimal Serving Temperature: 63° F
Vintage Year: 2014
Bottle Format: 750ml

Rastaban

Varietals: Pinot Noir (100%)
Barrel Aging: 18 months in French oak
Skin Contact: 10-14 day
Type of Wine: Red
Alcohol: 13,3%
Optimal Serving Temperature: 63° F
Vintage Year: 2012
Bottle Format: 750ml

Ara

Varietals: Riesling (100%)
Barrel Aging: Stainless steel
Type of Wine: White
Alcohol: 13,8%
Optimal Serving Temperature: 50° F
Vintage Year: 2014
Bottle Format: 750ml

Sunny Mountain

Varietals: Pinot Noir (100%)
Barrel Aging: 18 months in oak; 80% new
Skin Contact: 10-14 day
Type of Wine: Red
Alcohol: 12,9%
Optimal Serving Temperature: 63° F
Vintage Year: 2010
Bottle Format: 750ml

Temperance Hill

Varietals: Pinot Noir (100%)
Barrel Aging: 18 months in French oak
Skin Contact: 10-14 day
Type of Wine: Red
Alcohol: 11,8%
Optimal Serving Temperature: 63° F
Vintage Year: 2010
Bottle Format: 750ml

Oak Ridge

Varietals: Gewürztraminer (100%)
Barrel Aging: Stainless steel
Type of Wine: White
Alcohol: 13,8%
Optimal Serving Temperature: 50° F
Vintage Year: 2012
Bottle Format: 750ml

Sweet P

Varietals: Riesling (100%)
Barrel Aging: Stainless steel
Type of Wine: White
Alcohol: 8,7%
Optimal Serving Temperature: 50° F
Vintage Year: 2013
Bottle Format: 750ml

KING ESTATE WINERY

Eugene, OREGON

www.kingestate.com
E-mail: info@kingestate.com
Address: 80854 Territorial Road,
Eugene, OR 97405
Phone: (503) 378-1526

HISTORY

The story of King Estate Winery dates back to 1979 when Ed King III moved to Oregon to enter the University of Oregon's MBA program just as Oregon's wine industry was beginning to blossom. Around that same time Ed's father, the late Ed King, Jr., founder of aviation electronics firm King Radio Corporation in Kansas, had sold his company and was developing an interest in wine through his travels. In 1991 his son, Ed, purchased a 600-acre ranch in southwest Eugene near Lorane, Oregon, and enlisted his father's support in transforming the property into a large-scale winery. The first grapes were planted in 1992 on just 16.5 acres. By 1994, more than 100 acres were planted primarily in Pinot Gris and Pinot Noir to create the most clonally diverse soil and climate-matched vineyard ever grown in Oregon. The first harvest of estate-grown grapes was in 1995 and totaled 20 tons. Over time the company acquired two adjoining properties, bringing the total size to 1,033 acres with 470 planted to vine. The highly acclaimed King Estate Restaurant, adjoining the winery to the north, opened in May 2006. That same year the company, recognizing the high quality and bright future of Washington State's wine industry, developed its North by Northwest label featuring wines from the Columbia Valley and Walla Walla regions.

OWNERSHIP & MANAGEMENT

To this day King Estate is owned and operated by the King family, starting with Ed King Jr.'s children, Michelle King Theis and Ed King III, who is CEO and Co-Founder. Ed's wife, Jodee King, sons Justin, Taylor and Joe King and nephew Charles Theis are all active in the day-to-day operations of the winery in various capacities. Brent Stone, who joined King Estate in 2011, was named Winemaker in 2016 and added Chief Operating Officer to his duties in

2018. As COO he works closely with the CEO to oversee winery operations. Raymond Nuclo joined King Estate in 2013 and is Director of Viticulture and Winery Operations, overseeing viticulture, winemaking operations and contracts with vineyard partners. One of King Estate's original workers, Meliton Martinez, is now Vineyard Manager. Nigel Francisco is Chief Financial Officer and Justin King is National Sales Manager.

WINEMAKER
Brent Stone has over 15 years of industry experience. He began his career as an R&D chemist and managed food laboratories and quality assurance programs for several years in the dairy industry. Brent joined King Estate as the Lab Manager in 2011 and quickly gained an appreciation for wine. He received formal training in Enology at Washington State University and became a Winemaker at King Estate in 2016. In 2018 his role expanded to include Chief Operating Officer where he oversees all aspects of the winery operations including bottling, packaging, supply chain and product development. He is currently completing graduate work in agricultural food and life sciences at the University of Arkansas.

VINEYARD
The winery owns 1,033 acres of land, out of which 470 acres are under vine. King Estate was certified as Biodynamic by Demeter USA in 2016, making it the largest Biodynamic vineyard in the United States. At King Estate, with relatively high elevation, they have primarily two kinds of soil from two different sources: Bellpine soil is what's known as marine

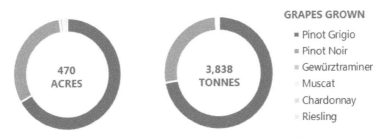

470 ACRES

3,838 TONNES

GRAPES GROWN
- Pinot Grigio
- Pinot Noir
- Gewürztraminer
- Muscat
- Chardonnay
- Riesling

sedimentary, formed when Oregon was under the sea more than 12 million years ago; and Jory soil is volcanic, created by more recent lava flows, relatively speaking, that date back six million to 15 million years. These Bellpine and Jory clay-loam soils are rich in iron, well draining, with excellent moisture retention requiring no additional irrigation.

Their stainless steel white wine tanks, ranging in size from 600 to 9,000 gallons, are where settling and fermentation take place. They ferment at about 55° F. The juice is first settled for 24 to 48 hours. Clean juice is racked off the solids and moved to another closed-top tank for fermentation. It takes about 45 to 60 days to complete the fermentation. Red wine fermentation is similar except they destem the berries. All lots are kept separate by tank. They usually cold soak at 40° F for a few days in an open-top tank before inoculating with cultured yeast. The grapes are transferred into the open-top fermenters where punch-downs are performed twice daily. Fermentation is in the classic Burgundian-style at a slightly cooler temperature around 82° F and lasts for 10 days to two weeks.

King Estate wines are available at their tasting room, and are distributed to retailers and restaurants across the United States.

Top restaurants that serve King Estate Wines

1. Bern's Steakhouse, Tampa, FL
2. Soho House, New York, NY
3. Duke's Chowder House, Seattle, WA
4. Kevin Rathburn Steak, Atlanta, GA
5. Spago, Beverly Hills, CA
6. Fontainebleu, Miami, FL
7. Perry's Steakhouse, Dallas, T
8. Shaw's Crab House, Chicago, IL
9. Joe's Seafood, Las Vegas, NV
10. Season's 52, Mutliple locations nationally

VISITOR INFORMATION
The winery and tasting room can be visited without appointment. Tours and tastings are available at a cost. Group tours (maximum 20 people) are also available. The winery receives about 20,000 visitors annually, and is also available for private events.

WINES

Pinot Gris - Willamette Valley

Varietals: Pinot Gris (100%)
Type of Wine: White
Alcohol: 13,5%
Optimal Serving Temperature: 50° F
Vintage Year: 2017
Bottle Format: 750ml
Awards: Gold Medal, Houston Rodeo Uncorked Wine Competition; Double Gold Medal, Savor NW Wine Competition

Pinot Noir - Willamette Valley

Varietals: Pinot Noir (100%)
Barrel aging: 8-10 months in French oak
Skin Contact: 14 days
Type of Wine: Red
Alcohol: 13,5%
Optimal Serving Temperature: 62° F
Vintage Year: 2016
Bottle Format: 750ml
Awards: Gold Medal, San Francisco Chronicle Wine Competition

Rosé of Pinot Noir

Varietals: Pinot Noir (100%)
Skin Contact: 2 days
Type of Wine: Rosé
Alcohol: 13,5%
Optimal Serving Temperature: 50° F
Vintage Year: 2018
Bottle Format: 750ml
Awards: Gold Medal, Savor NW Wine Competition

Pinot Gris - Domaine

Varietals: Pinot Gris (100%)
Type of Wine: White
Alcohol: 13,5%
Optimal Serving Temperature: 50° F
Vintage Year: 2017
Bottle Format: 750ml
Awards: Double Gold Medal, Houston Rodeo Uncorked Wine Competition; Gold Medal, San Francisco Chronicle Wine Competition

Pinot Noir - Domaine

Varietals: Pinot Noir (100%)
Barrel aging: 18 months in French oak; 26% new
Skin Contact: 14 days
Type of Wine: Red
Alcohol: 13,5%
Optimal Serving Temperature: 62° F
Vintage Year: 2015
Bottle Format: 750ml
Awards: Silver Medal, San Francisco Chronicle Wine Competition; Silver Medal, Critics Challenge International Wine & Spirits Competition

Chardonnay

Varietals: Chardonnay (100%)
Barrel aging: 5 months in French oak
Type of Wine: White
Alcohol: 13,5%
Optimal Serving Temperature: 50° F
Vintage Year: 2017
Bottle Format: 750ml

ST. INNOCENT WINERY

Jefferson, OREGON

www.stinnocentwine.com
E-mail: mark@stinnocentwine.com
Address: 10052 Enchanted Way SE,
Jefferson, OR 97352
Phone: (503) 378-1526

HISTORY

Mark Vlossak founded St. Innocent Winery in 1988. At that time, wine grapes in Oregon were primarily grown by vineyards with no associated winery, similar to the model in Burgundy. Today, most of Oregon's most famous vineyards still have no associated winery. The growers lease specific parcels of their vineyards to wineries that then produce vineyard designated wines. St. Innocent Winery has always worked under this model; searching for great sites and leasing grapes from specific blocks to make its wines. The winery has been blessed with Mark's vineyard choices. A recent feature "Five Great Oregon Vineyards" noted that St. Innocent Winery was the only Oregon winery to produce wine from all five of those great sites.

Over their 31 years, St. Innocent Winery has made wine in four locations. Their final move was the purchase of a 47.5-acre parcel in the South Salem Hills that is named Enchanted Way Vineyard. The new winery features gravity flow, a naturally cooled underground barrel room and a seamless integration with the surrounding vineyard. They have a tasting room, a large deck and outdoor patios that are open daily. They will add Chardonnay from Enchanted Way Vineyard to their four vineyard designated Pinot Noirs.

OWNERSHIP & MANAGEMENT

St. Innocent Winery is a corporation founded in 1988. There were nine original stockholders, of which five are still involved. Mark Vlossak, who owns 66% of the stock, acts as CEO, President, Treasurer, as well as Winemaker. Mark oversees the farming, all aspects

of winemaking and distribution. After over 30 years of winemaking Mark is a true vigneron, overseeing the vineyard from planting to finished wine. His wife, Vickianne, joined him five years ago and manages the Direct to Consumer portion of the business. On any given day you can run into one or both of the Vlossaks on site.

WINEMAKER

Mark Vlossak began his exploration of wine at an early age. His father, a wine importer, tasted wines with him from the time he was seven years old. His mother loved to cook and took classes with the Madame Kuony, a graduate of France's Le Cordon Bleu. Thus, his love of wine and food became an integral part of his personality. Not only was this key to training his palate, it also cultivated the idea that wine is food and wines are meant to be enjoyed with food.

After moving to Oregon, he was drawn to Oregon's wine industry which, at that time, was in its infancy. He

attended extension seminars at University of California, Davis' wine program. From 1997 to 1999, Mark apprenticed with Oregon wine pioneer, Fred Arterberry. He founded St. Innocent Winery in 1988. In honor of his father, who helped train Mark's palate, the winery is named after him using his middle name "Innocent". Mark's vision was to make wines that respect the quality and tradition of the Old World in the new grape growing region of Oregon's Willamette Valley. Specifically, he set out to make single vineyard designated Pinot Noirs from areas around the Willamette Valley that would have distinctive personalities and pair with a wide variety of foods. Thirty-one harvests later, Mark has achieved his goal as one of Oregon's most lauded winemakers. He produces single vineyard designated wines including Pinot Noir, Pinot Blanc and Chardonnay from six of Oregon's most well known vineyards. His wines enhance and prolong the pleasure of a meal.

VINEYARD

The winery owns 48 acres of land and leases another 41 acres, out of which 56 acres are under vine. The backbone of their production is vineyard designated wines from four of Oregon's greatest terroirs: Shea, Freedom Hill, Temperance Hill and Momtazi Vineyards. They purchased Enchanted Way Vineyard in the South Salem Hills in 2018. It is planted with eight acres of Chardonnay and seven acres of Pinot Noir. Soils in Oregon's Willamette Valley fall into two categories; those of volcanic origin and those of sedimentary origin. St. Innocent works with vineyards with both of these soil types.

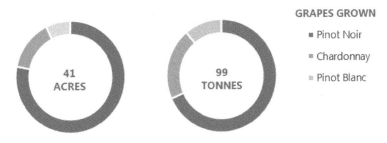

GRAPES GROWN

- Pinot Noir
- Chardonnay
- Pinot Blanc

41 ACRES

99 TONNES

Pinot Noir grapes are hand-picked and immediately processed at the winery. The bunches are 100% destemmed. They use 30% to 40% whole berries and add no SO_2 to the must. The fermentations begin around 12° C and are allowed to warm naturally to about 30° to 34° C. Punch-downs are done by hand only once a day, and only when the fermentation is active. The wines are pressed based on the tannin balance of each lot. After 3 to 5 days of settling, the young wine is racked to French oak barrels with 15% to 28% new barrels. Aging in barrel continues for 15 to 16 months in a naturally temperature-controlled cellar underground. Finally the barrels are bottled by gravity. None of their wines are fined, so no proteins are added and all the wines are vegan.

St. Innocent wines are available at their tasting room, via their website and at retail wine shops and restaurants. The wines are also exported to Canada and Germany.

Top restaurants that serve St. Innocent Wines

1. Gramercy Tavern, New York, NY
2. A Rake's Progress, Washington, DC
3. Black Salt, Washington, DC
4. Peninsula Grill, Charleston, SC
5. The Painted Lady, Newburg, OR
6. Zoe's Restaurant, Virginia Beach, VA
7. Ringside Restaurant, Portland, OR
8. Portland City Grill, Portland, OR
9. 9 Park, Boston, MA
10. The Jefferson Hotel, Richmond, VA

VISITOR INFORMATION
The winery and tasting room can be visited without appointment. Tours and tastings are available at a cost. The winery offers group tours (maximum 10 people) and is also available for private events.

WINES

Chardonnay - Freedom Hill Vineyard

Varietals: Chardonnay (100%)
Barrel Aging: 11 months in French oak
Type of Wine: White
Alcohol: 14,0%
Optimal Serving Temperature: 48° F
Vintage Year: 2016
Bottle Format: 750ml

Pinot Noir - Freedom Hill Vineyard

Varietals: Pinot Noir (100%)
Barrel aging: 16 months in French oak; 27% new
Skin Contact: 12-15 days
Type of Wine: Red
Alcohol: 13,5%
Optimal Serving Temperature: 65° F
Vintage Year: 2015
Bottle Format: 750ml

Pinot Noir – Momtazi Vineyard

Varietals: Pinot Noir (100%)
Barrel aging: 16 months in French oak; 28% new
Skin Contact: 12-15 days
Type of Wine: Red
Alcohol: 13,5%
Optimal Serving Temperature: 65° F
Vintage Year: 2015
Bottle Format: 750ml

Pinot Blanc - Freedom Hill Vineyard

Varietals: Pinot Blanc (100%)
Barrel Aging: 8 months
Type of Wine: White
Alcohol: 12,5%
Optimal Serving Temperature: 48° F
Vintage Year: 2015
Bottle Format: 750ml

Pinot Noir - Temperance Hill Vineyard

Varietals: Pinot Noir (100%)
Barrel aging: 16 months in French oak; 21% new
Skin Contact: 12-15 days
Type of Wine: Red
Alcohol: 13,2%
Optimal Serving Temperature: 65° F
Vintage Year: 2015
Bottle Format: 750ml

Pinot Noir – Shea Vineyard

Varietals: Pinot Noir (100%)
Barrel aging: 16 months in French oak; 25% new
Skin Contact: 12-15 days
Type of Wine: Red
Alcohol: 13,5%
Optimal Serving Temperature: 65° F
Vintage Year: 2015
Bottle Format: 750ml

St. Innocent Winery Photos by Andréa Johnson Photography

STAG HOLLOW WINES

Yamhill, OREGON

www.staghollow.com
E-mail: staghollow@staghollow.com
Address: 7930 NE Blackburn Road,
Yamhill, Oregon 97148
Phone: (503) 662-5609

HISTORY

With an enthusiasm for many types of wine and after bicycling the vineyards of Europe during their honeymoon, Mark Huff and Jill Zarnowitz discovered and purchased 34 acres of rolling pasture and woodland near the towns of Yamhill and Carlton, Oregon. Planting of Pommard and Colmar 538 Pinot Noir clones began in 1990. Over several years, 10 acres of Pinot Noir, Muscat Ottonel, Early Muscat, Dolcetto and Tempranillo were planted. With a passion for complex and full-flavored Pinot Noir that aged, Mark and Jill planted Pinot Noir at over 3,000 vines per acre to moderately stress the plants. To attain this, Mark developed a unique trellis system positioning grape shoots downward to accentuate moderate vine stress and cluster exposure to sunlight, which concentrate flavors and enhances wine complexity. Wine production at Stag Hollow began with the 1994 vintage producing a long-lived intense Pinot Noir that still gives pleasure today. With their substantial work in ecology and fish and wildlife conservation, Mark and Jill manage their vineyard and winery at a small boutique level. Small scale grape-growing and wine production have given Jill and Mark the freedom to focus on wine quality that expresses their meticulous vineyard practices and distinct terroir.

OWNERSHIP & MANAGEMENT

Through knowledge gained in his doctoral studies and work in ecological sciences, Mark has applied his understanding of the environment to practices in the vineyard. Stag Hollow

grapes are grown as part of a larger ecosystem, next to streams, wetlands, forests and oak savannahs that provide habitat for diverse wildlife populations. Mark is hands-on in the vineyard and hands-off in the winery. Understanding what a piece of land is capable of, producing over 30 years and what tweaks need to be done to improve quality in the vineyard have been richly rewarding for Mark. The most important step in the annual grape-growing process is to determine when to harvest each grape variety and vineyard block; these decisions are not data-driven, rather they are accomplished by tasting the grapes to determine when optimal flavor profiles have developed that can translate into compelling wines.

Equipped with a Master's of Science in Wildlife Biology and working two decades on wildlife conservation with Oregon's Department of Fish and Wildlife, Jill Zarnowitz is the inspirational force behind Stag Hollow Vineyard being maintained as a "working" ecological reserve. Jill, Board member of the Yamhill-Carlton "American Viticultural Area," administers Stag Hollow wine and vineyard operations with her golden lab, Brix, at her side.

VINEYARD
The winery owns 34 acres of land, out of which 10 acres are under vine. The soil at Stag Hollow is Willakenzie, which is moderately shallow on the slopes planted with grapes. Formed from sandstone, siltstone and tuffaceous materials, this soil is hailed for making dark, richly textured Pinot Noirs with layered blueberry-cherry notes. The Wilakenzie soil is

GRAPES GROWN

- Pinot Noir
- Dolcetto
- Muscat
- Tempranillo

10 ACRES

18 TONNES

characterized by 5 to 10 inches of shallow dark brown loam, followed by a yellowish-brown loam with a blocky structure that eventually becomes dense and often seamed with white or yellowish clay.

Stag Hollow grapes are lightly crushed, destemmed, and fermented in 1-ton covered fermentation vats. Often, dry ice is used to cool the crushed grapes to retain fruit characteristics. Cold soaks of grapes skins on the juice usually last about 4 days before fermentation. The grape must is fermented at cool temperatures, at or under 80°F, finishing usually in 14 to 20 days. After fermentation is complete, the wine and grape skins are emptied into a grape press. Free-run juice is collected first and transferred into 60-gallon French or Oregon oak barrels, and then the pressed juice is moved into separate barrels. Wines are barrel-aged 6 months on the yeast lees to add complexity and richness, then racked off the lees in April, and bottled after 11 months. Pinot Noir is aged in 15 to 30% new oak barrels and bottled-aged one to four years before release.

Stag Hollow wines are available at their tasting room, via their website and in grocery stores, wine shops and restaurants throughout Oregon.

Top restaurants that serve Stag Hollow Wines

1. Purple Café, Seattle, Bellevue, Woodinville, WA
2. The Joel Palmer House, Dayton, OR
3. Tina's Restaurant, Dundee, OR

VISITOR INFORMATION
The winery and tasting room can be visited with prior appointment. Group tours (maximum 15 people) are available.

WINES

Reserve 777-114 Pinot Noir

Varietals: Pinot Noir (100%)
Barrel aging: 11 months in French oak
Skin Contact: 14-20 days
Type of Wine: Red
Alcohol: 14,5%
Optimal Serving Temperature: 63° F
Vintage Year: 2014
Bottle Format: 750ml

Pinot Noir

Varietals: Pinot Noir (100%)
Barrel aging: 10 months in French oak
Skin Contact: 10 days
Type of Wine: Red
Alcohol: 14,5%
Optimal Serving Temperature: 63° F
Vintage Year: 2014
Bottle Format: 750ml

Vendange Sélection Pinot Noir

Varietals: Pinot Noir (100%)
Barrel aging: 10 months in French oak
Skin Contact: 10 days
Type of Wine: Red
Alcohol: 14,5%
Optimal Serving Temperature: 63° F
Vintage Year: 2014
Bottle Format: 750ml

Dolcetto

Varietals: Dolcetto (100%)
Barrel aging: 10 months in French and American oak
Skin Contact: 10 days
Type of Wine: Red
Alcohol: 13,0%
Optimal Serving Temperature: 63° F
Vintage Year: 2014
Bottle Format: 750ml

Reserve Pinot Noir

Varietals: Pinot Noir (100%)
Barrel aging: 10 months in French oak
Skin Contact: 10 days
Type of Wine: Red
Alcohol: 14,5%
Optimal Serving Temperature: 63° F
Vintage Year: 2015
Bottle Format: 750ml

Tempranillo

Varietals: Tempranillo (100%)
Barrel aging: 10 months in French oak
Skin Contact: 10 days
Type of Wine: Red
Alcohol: 14,5%
Optimal Serving Temperature: 63° F
Vintage Year: 2015
Bottle Format: 750ml

Vendange Sélection Pinot Noir

Varietals: Pinot Noir (100%)
Barrel aging: 10 months in French oak
Skin Contact: 10 days
Type of Wine: Red
Alcohol: 14,5%
Optimal Serving Temperature: 63° F
Vintage Year: 2015
Bottle Format: 750ml

Stag Hollow Photos by RJ Studios

SWEET CHEEKS WINERY

Eugene, OREGON

www.sweetcheekswinery.com
E-mail: info@sweetcheekswinery.com
Address: 27007 Briggs Hill Road,
Eugene OR 97405
Phone: (541) 349-9463

HISTORY

Our story began in the early 1980's when owner, Dan Smith planted a vineyard on a rolling hillside in Crow, Oregon. After a hard day of work he looked over the vineyard and noticed the curious shape of the land and christened the vineyard Sweet Cheeks. At this point starting a winery was only a dream. He continued to farm the land, supplying Pinot Noir, Pinot Gris, Chardonnay and Riesling grapes to local wineries. When a building in Junction City came up for demolition in 2003 he took a chance and relocated it atop the vineyard. Thanksgiving of 2005 the doors opened as their tasting room and marked the beginning of Sweet Cheeks Winery & Vineyard.

OWNERSHIP & MANAGEMENT

With the loss of leader and visionary owner, Dan Smith, in 2018 the torch was passed to his wife, Beth Smith, and the Winemaker, Leo Gabica. Leo was the first employee ever hired at Sweet Cheeks Winery, working in the cellar until he became the Winemaker in 2013. Dan's granddaughter, Jessica Thomas is the winery's General Manager.

WINEMAKER

Originally from the Philippines, Leo moved to Oregon in 1994 to work for a family rock crushing business. He answered an advertisement for a neighboring winery to help with the bottling lines, and fell in love with the industry. He learned by working with some of the most respected winemakers in the Oregon wine industry. In the early 2000's Dan Smith offered Leo a position at Sweet Cheeks Winery to work in the cellar. Leo completed his first vintage as lead Winemaker in 2013. He is very active in the community, and spends all of

his time outside of the winery with his family composed of wife, Gina, his three kids, Ivy, Ian and Imari, and Grandson, Isaiah.

VINEYARD

The winery owns 55 acres of land, out of which 42 acres are under vine. Willakenzie soil is the primary soil in the vineyard. The soil is usually moist, but dry for 45 to 60 days of the year between the depths of 4 to 12 feet following the summer solstice. This causes the roots to explore and create a very large root system. They also have steiwer soil in the southern-most point of the vineyard where the Kody block Pinot Noir, Chardonnay and Horse Pinot Gris grows.

For whites, after whole-cluster processing, the juice is put to tank at 45° F for about 4 to 5 days. During this time the heavy sediment in the juice is allowed to settle. Once the juice is clear it is racked off the lees and gradually warmed to about 60°. At 60° the tank is inoculated with conventional yeast. For whites, the temperature during fermentation is anywhere from 50° to 55° F depending how active the ferment is. Usually they want the brix to drop about a 1 brix per day. If the drop is more than 1.5 brix the temperature is lowered to slow yeast activity. This allows whites to maintain aromatics. Most of their whites are stainless steel fermented. Most whites take about a month to finish fermentation.

GRAPES GROWN

42 ACRES

153 TONNES

- Pinot Noir
- Pinot Grigio
- Riesling
- Chardonnay

For reds, the fruits are destemmed and allowed to go through cold soaking at 40° to 45° F for 3 to 5 days then will gradually be warmed to 72° F before inoculation. Fermentation temperature is between 72° F and 85° F. During fermentation, they are two ways of cap management, punch-down and pump-over. The fermentation of the reds usually last about a week to a week and a half. When alcoholic fermentation is completed the wine is pressed off from the skins and put to barrel where it undergoes to malolactic fermentation.

Sweet Cheeks wines are available at their two tasting rooms; one at the winery on Briggs Hill and the other at The Fifth Street Public Market in Eugene, Oregon. The wines are also available in Oregon and in select areas in Washington, Louisiana and Florida.

Top restaurants that serve Sweet Cheeks Wines

1. Papa's Pizza, Eugene, OR
2. Back Alley, Noth Bend, OR
3. Il Terrazzo, Portland, OR
4. Hop Valley Brewing Co., Eugene, OR
5. 1285 Restobar, Florence, OR
6. Friendly Food Bar & Deli, Eugene, OR
7. Bill & Tim's Barbecue, Eugene, OR
8. Ocean Bleu Seafoods, Newport, OR
9. B2 Wine Bar, Eugene, OR
10. 503 Uncorked, Sherwood, OR

VISITOR INFORMATION
The winery and tasting rooms can be visited without appointment. Tastings are available at a cost. The winery is available for private events.

WINES

Pinot Noir

Varietals: Pinot Noir (100%)
Barrel Aging: 9 months in French oak; 28% new
Skin Contact: 3 days
Type of Wine: Red
Alcohol: 13,9%
Optimal Serving Temperature: 63° F
Vintage Year: 2016
Bottle Format: 750ml

Pinot Gris

Varietals: Pinot Gris (100%)
Barrel Aging: Stainless steel
Type of Wine: White
Alcohol: 13,5%
Optimal Serving Temperature: 53° F
Vintage Year: 2016
Bottle Format: 750ml

Vintage Riesling

Varietals: Riesling (100%)
Barrel Aging: Stainless steel
Type of Wine: White
Alcohol: 10,0%
Optimal Serving Temperature: 53° F
Vintage Year: 2016
Bottle Format: 750ml
Awards: Silver Medal, 2017 New Orleans
International Wine Competition; Silver Medal,
2017 San Francisco Chronicle Wine Competition

Pinot Fusion

Varietals: Pinot Noir (39%), Syrah (32%), Merlot
(29%)
Barrel Aging: 11 months in French oak
Skin Contact: 3-5 days
Type of Wine: Red
Alcohol: 13,5%
Optimal Serving Temperature: 63° F
Vintage Year: 2015
Bottle Format: 750ml

Chardonnay

Varietals: Chardonnay (100%)
Barrel Aging: 14 months in French oak; 22% new
Type of Wine: White
Alcohol: 12,3%
Optimal Serving Temperature: 53° F
Vintage Year: 2016
Bottle Format: 750ml

Sauvignon Blanc

Varietals: Sauvignon Blanc (100%)
Barrel Aging: Stainless steel
Type of Wine: White
Alcohol: 13,0%
Optimal Serving Temperature: 53° F
Vintage Year: 2017
Bottle Format: 750ml
Awards: Silver Medal, 2017 San Francisco
Chronicle Wine Competition

TYEE WINE CELLARS

Corvallis, OREGON

www.tyeewine.com
E-mail: info@www.tyeewine.com
Address: 26335 Greenberry Road,
Corvallis OR 97333
Phone: (541) 241-8933

HISTORY

Tyee Wine Cellars is located on the scenic Buchanan Family Century Farm founded over 130 years ago in the heart of Oregon's Willamette Valley near Corvallis. Tyee founders, Dave and Margy Buchanan planted the first Tyee Estate wine grapes in 1974, and Tyee Wine Cellars' first commercial vintage was in 1985.

OWNERSHIP & MANAGEMENT

Today the family farm is operated cooperatively by fourth and fifth generation family farmers. The farm remains a diverse operation, with an estate vineyard and winery, tasting parlor and historic barn, events facility, hiking trails and picnic tables through hazelnut orchards, cathedral oak trees and Willamette Valley native woodlands and wetlands. Visitors to Tyee Wine Cellars are welcome to enjoy wine tasting and picnicking on the family farm and vineyard in a variety of scenic locations or hikes along Tyee's Beaver Pond Loop Nature Trail and conservation easement.

Tyee is a small, family owned and operated winery, with a limited production of 2,000 cases annually. Tyee's Winemaker, Merrilee Buchanan Benson, is a fifth generation Willamette Valley farmer who grew up with the vines. She and her husband, Brian Benson, manage Tyee Estate Vineyard and the traditional winemaking process at Tyee to create Tyee Estate Pinot Gris, Chardonnay Gewurztraminer and Pinot Noir.

Merrilee planted wine grapes in Tyee Estate Vineyard starting in the 1980's and all the way through to the last planting in 2014. She studied organic and biodynamic farming methods and sustainable viticultural practices to integrate into her farming methods. She believes that wine is made in the vineyard and works with her husband Brian to use a no till farming method, using only organically approved materials as inputs in the vineyard in a way that is friendly to wildlife and biodiversity.

VINEYARD

The winery owns 15 acres of land, all of which is under vine. Tyee Estate Vineyard is located in the Willamette Valley AVA, just about a mile away from the Willamette River on the first terrace off the valley floor. Elevation is 300 feet and the soil type is Willamette, a silty clay loam. The vineyard is south facing and is farmed with a no-till method to increase soil life and plant biodiversity, sequester carbon, decrease erosion and naturally balance the grape vine canopy for increased sunlight and airflow. Only organically approved materials are added to the vineyard. All Tyee Estate Wines are entirely grown, produced, and bottled at Tyee so each wine expresses the unique terroir of the Tyee Estate Vineyard.

At Tyee Wine Cellars they use native yeast that naturally comes in on the grapes harvested from Tyee Estate Vineyard especially in Tyee Estate Pinot Noir and also use added yeasts especially in Tyee Estate White Wines. They use small batch fermentors and relatively cool peak fermentation temperatures to achieve the best fruit forward flavors and aromatics in their wines. Fermentors of whole cluster and whole berry Pinot Noir are gently hand punched down daily by the winemakers.

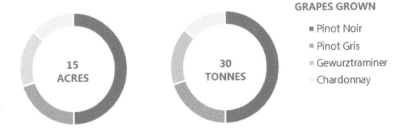

15 ACRES

30 TONNES

GRAPES GROWN

- Pinot Noir
- Pinot Gris
- Gewurztraminer
- Chardonnay

Tyee Estate Cellars wines are available at their tasting room, website and around Oregon, Colorado and Oklahoma.

Top restaurants that serve Tyee Estate Cellars Wines

1. Gathering Together Farm Restaurant, Philomath, OR
2. del Alma Restaurant, Corvallis, OR
3. Mazama Restaurant, Corvallis, OR
4. Nearly Normal's, Corvallis, OR
5. Table of Contents Restaurant at Sylvia Beach Hotel, Newport, OR
6. Local Ocean Seafoods, Newport, OR
7. Vault 244 Bistro, Albany, OR
8. North Fork Public House, Eugene, OR
9. Sushi Okalani, Hood River, OR
10. Fish Restaurant, Fort Collins, CO

VISITOR INFORMATION

The winery and tasting room can be visited without appointment. Tours and tastings are available at a cost. Group tours (maximum 50 people) are also available. The winery receives over 1,000 visitors annually and is also available for private events.

WINES

Tyee Estate Pinot Noir

Varietals: Pinot Noir (100%)
Barrel Aging: 18 months in French oak; 15% new
Skin Contact: 21 days
Type of Wine: Red
Alcohol: 13,5%
Optimal Serving Temperature: 60° F
Vintage Year: 2016
Bottle Format: 750ml

Tyee Estate Barrel Select Pinot Noir

Varietals: Pinot Noir (100%)
Barrel Aging: 18 months in French oak; 25% new
Skin Contact: 21 days
Type of Wine: Red
Alcohol: 13,5%
Optimal Serving Temperature: 60° F
Vintage Year: 2015
Bottle Format: 750ml

Tyee Estate Pinot Gris

Varietals: Pinot Gris (100%)
Barrel Aging: Stainless steel
Skin Contact: 3 days
Type of Wine: White
Alcohol: 13,5%
Optimal Serving Temperature: 40° F
Vintage Year: 2016
Bottle Format: 750ml

Tyee Estate Gewurztraminer

Varietals: Gewurztraminer (100%)
Barrel Aging: Stainless steel
Skin Contact: 24 hours
Type of Wine: White
Alcohol: 13,5%
Optimal Serving Temperature: 40° F
Vintage Year: 2016
Bottle Format: 750ml

Tyee Estate Chardonnay

Varietals: Chardonnay (100%)
Barrel Aging: Stainless steel
Skin Contact: 24 hours
Type of Wine: White
Alcohol: 13,5%
Optimal Serving Temperature: 40° F
Vintage Year: 2016
Bottle Format: 750ml

WILLAMETTE VALLEY VINEYARDS

Turner, OREGON

www.wvv.com
E-mail: info@wvv.com
Address: 8800 Enchanted Way SE
Turner, OR 97392
Phone: (503) 588-9463

HISTORY

The "budwood" of Willamette Valley Vineyards began long before its founding in 1983 by vintner Jim Bernau. His Dad, a Roseburg lawyer, was hired by a California winemaker to secure the first winery license in Oregon since Prohibition. Jim's Dad allowed small tastes of Richard Sommer's wine at the dinner table, lighting a path that led Jim from home winemaking to studies at University of California, Davis and eventually Beaune, France. His early "winemaking" grew more from mischief when at the age of 10, he liberated his Mom's frozen Concord grape juice from the freezer following the description of fermentation in the family's set of Encyclopedias.

In 1983, with the encouragement from winemakers making their move from California, Jim cleared away an old pioneer plum orchard in the Salem Hills, hidden underneath scotch broom and blackberry vines. Unable to afford drip irrigation, he watered them by hand using 17 lengths of 75 foot garden hose to get the grapelings through their first summer. Jim named it Willamette Valley Vineyards — later to become grandfathered into federal law when the American Viticultural Area was federally authorized.

Since the winery founding in 1983, stewardship of the land has been a key principle in the winemaking. Their approach is to grow by hand, the highest quality fruit using careful canopy management and yield balance, and to achieve wines that are truly expressive of the varietal and the place where they are grown. At Willamette Valley Vineyards, they practice environmentally sustainable farming and were part of the founding of the Low Input Viticulture and Enology Program.

OWNERSHIP & MANAGEMENT

In early days, founder Jim Bernau concentrated on helping Oregon Winegrowers by passing legislation on making wineries a permitted use on farmland, the direct shipment of wine, wine tastings in stores and restaurants, and later the establishment of the Oregon Wine

Board. Jim's personal gift to Oregon State
University established the first professorship for
fermentation science in the nation.

The recognition Jim values most came from his
fellow winegrowers when he involved in creating
the first system of environmental stewardship in
American agriculture, the Low Impact Viticulture
and Enology program, followed by awards
presented by the Rainforest Alliance and the
American Wine Society.

Jim believes among healthiest forms of business
organization are those owned by the
community. He conducted the first "crowd
funding" in the nation to build his winery by
obtaining permission from the Securities and
Exchange Commission in 1988, resulting in a
growing fabric of laws allowing community-
based funding for small businesses.

Winery Director, Christine Clair's love for
Oregon wine began at an early age looking up

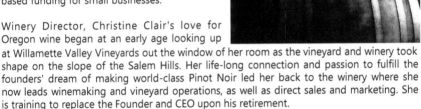

at Willamette Valley Vineyards out the window of her room as the vineyard and winery took
shape on the slope of the Salem Hills. Her life-long connection and passion to fulfill the
founders' dream of making world-class Pinot Noir led her back to the winery where she
now leads winemaking and vineyard operations, as well as direct sales and marketing. She
is training to replace the Founder and CEO upon his retirement.

WINEMAKER
Head Winemaker Joe Ibrahim knew from a very early age that he was destined for a career
in viticulture and enology. Joe decided to study Plant and Soil Science at the University of
Vermont. After graduating college, he accepted a position with Ste. Michelle Wine Estate in
Washington State, where he learned about making wine in the Pacific Northwest. He was
later offered a position with Gallo Family in California where he learned about brandy
distillation as a Spirits Maker and sparkling wine production as the Senior Winemaker in
charge of the sparkling wine program.

He came to discover that his true passion is in crafting premium cool climate varieties like
Pinot Noir and Chardonnay. As the Head Winemaker for Edna Valley Vineyard, in one of
California's coolest AVA's, he crafted premium and luxury wines and developed a reputation
for creating award winning wines from some of the region's most iconic vineyard sites. Jim
Bernau invited Joe to visit Willamette Valley Vineyards and he instantly knew he had found
his new home.

VINEYARD
The winery owns almost 596 acres of land, and leases another 317 acres, out of which 330
acres are under vine. The Willamette Valley is a fertile triangular region of more than 100
miles long and up to 60 miles wide. The Valley climate provides an elongated grape-
growing season that is said to be ideal for Pinot Noir. Winter is typically cool, wet and mild.
Spring is oftentimes rainy, and summers are warm with cool evenings. An important
distinction is the Willamette Valley location on the global 45th area is considered to be an
ideal climate for viniferous grape growing; it is said to provide the ideal balance of
temperature, humidity and soil. The Jory and Nekia soils at the Willamette Valley Vineyards
Estate in Turner, Oregon are well drained to a depth of one and a half to six feet.

Their general practices for Estate and Single Vineyard Pinot Noir fermentations is to gently
destem, with approximately 90% of the berries remaining intact for whole berry

GRAPES GROWN
- Pinot Noir
- Pinot Grigio
- Chardonnay
- Riesling
- Muscat
- Pinot Blanc
- Gruner Veltliner

fermentation, which adds lively fruit characteristics. Prior to fermentation they use non-saccharmycese cerevisiae yeast strain, which provides improved complexity, color and mouthfeel. On the fifth day, the must is inoculated with indigenous yeast. After 8 to 12 days of fermentation in small fermenters and manual punch-downs, the must is pressed out with about 1% residual sugar and is allowed to settle in the tank overnight. They barrel the new wine with light, fluffy lees where it finishes primary fermentation and undergoes malolactic fermentation.

Willamette Valley Vineyards wines are available nationally in many chain retail outlets, independent grocery and bottle shops, national chain restaurants and independent restaurants.

Top restaurants that serve Willamette Valley Vineyards Wines

1. Olive Garden, Multiple locations in Oregon
2. J Alexander's, Multiple locations nationally
3. PF Chang's, Multiple locations nationally
4. Kona Grill, Multiple locations nationally
5. Pappadeaux, Multiple locations nationally
6. Fleming's Prime Rib, Multiple locations nationally
7 Ruth's Chris Steakhouse, Multiple locations nationally
8. Chart House Restaurants, Multiple locations nationally
9. Pine Tavern, Bend, OR
10. Sunriver Brewing, Bend, OR

VISITOR INFORMATION
The winery and tasting room can be visited without appointment. Tastings and tours are available at a cost. The winery also offers group tours (maximum 55 people) and is also available for private events.

WINES

Estate Pinot Noir

Varietals: Pinot Noir (100%)
Barrel Aging: 9 months in French oak; 25% new
Type of Wine: Red
Alcohol: 13,9%
Vintage Year: 2016
Bottle Format: 750ml

Brut

Varietals: Pinot Noir (60%), Chardonnay (40%)
Barrel Aging: 18 months
Type of Wine: White
Alcohol: 12,8%
Vintage Year: 2015
Bottle Format: 750ml

Whole Cluster Rosé of Pinot Noir

Varietals: Pinot Noir (100%)
Barrel Aging: Stainless steel
Type of Wine: Rosé
Alcohol: 13,5%
Vintage Year: 2017
Bottle Format: 750ml

Estate Chardonnay

Varietals: Chardonnay (100%)
Barrel Aging: 10 months in French oak; 25% new
Type of Wine: White
Alcohol: 13,9%
Vintage Year: 2016
Bottle Format: 750ml

Whole Cluster Pinot Noir

Varietals: Pinot Noir (100%)
Barrel Aging: Stainless steel
Type of Wine: Red
Alcohol: 13,5%
Vintage Year: 2017
Bottle Format: 750ml

Bernau Block Pinot Noir

Varietals: Pinot Noir (100%)
Barrel Aging: 15 months in French oak; 27% new
Type of Wine: Red
Alcohol: 14,1%
Vintage Year: 2015
Bottle Format: 750ml

YOUNGBERG HILL

McMinnville, OREGON

www.youngberghill.com
E-mail: info@youngberghill.com
Address: 10660 SW Youngberg Hill
Road, McMinnville, OR 97128
Phone: (503) 472-2727

HISTORY

Wayne Bailey and his wife Nicolette treasured a childhood growing up on a farm in Iowa and the qualities and life lessons it gave. They wanted the same for their three daughters; Natasha, Jordan and Aspen. With the future in mind they wanted to create a sustainable and responsible farm. That is why they started farming organically in 2003 and continue to move toward biodynamic practices. Youngberg Hill is a small, family estate grower and producer of Oregon Pinot Noir and Pinot Gris. Oregon's premier wine country estate, set on a 50-acre hilltop surrounded by exquisite vineyards and views, Youngberg Hill, has an amazing 29-year old vineyard. The estate is owned by the Bailey family and is well known for producing award-winning wines. As passionate farmers and winemakers they are thrilled to share, educate and talk wine. In addition, they have a 9-room Inn for the perfect retreat, and are centrally located in the Willamette Valley.

OWNERSHIP & MANAGEMENT

Wayne and Nicolette Bailey purchased Youngberg Hill in 2003 and overhauled the entire estate, including vineyard management, winemaking, tasting room and hospitality. With backgrounds in winemaking, distribution, food & beverage, hospitality and marketing, they knew that all of their talents would be used to turn something that was already beautiful on the outside into a place that was equally as beautiful on the inside, too.

VINEYARD

The winery owns 50 acres of land, out of which approximately 20 acres are under vine. They have three distinct blocks of Pinot Noir and one block of Pinot Gris and Chardonnay. The Natasha block at 6.5 acres is the largest of the three Pinot Noir blocks, and is located at an elevation of approximately 600 feet on marine sedimentary soil. The Jordan block of Pinot Noir is 5 acres in area and grows on a steep slope of volcanic rock at an altitude of approximately 750 to 800 feet. Both blocks are own-rooted 60% pommard and 40% wadenswil clones, planted in 1989. The Bailey block, Dijon 777 on 10114 root stock, is their third block of Pinot Noir planted in 2008, has an area of 3.5 acres located between the Jordan and Natasha blocks. It grows in primarily volcanic rock with a wide band of shale running through the middle about 18 inches down. The Aspen block, planted in 2006, consists of 2.5 acres of Pinot Gris, 148 and 152 clones on 3309 root stock at approximately 525 to 600 feet; and 2.5 acres of Chardonnay, 75, 76, 95, and 548 clones on the same root stock. These clones are more suited to ripen in their cooler climate.

Founded in 1989, Youngberg Hill aspires to create the very best wine from the grapes grown in each vintage. They focus their attention on growing the highest quality of grapes possible and then managing the fruit through the fermentation process. By limiting yields and restraining barrel treatment, they are able to produce fine wines that give a pure expression of the beautiful vineyard and its terroir. The attentive grower watches over the vines as nature works its miracles, feeling the energy of life in the air and tending the vineyard sensitively and with a light hand. They aim to bring out the potential of the grapes and to let the story of this place- the terroir of the vineyard and the year of the vintage- be told with clarity in the wine.

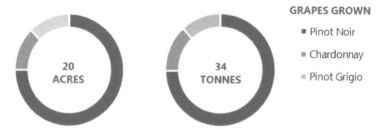

GRAPES GROWN

- Pinot Noir
- Chardonnay
- Pinot Grigio

20 ACRES

34 TONNES

Youngberg Hill wines are available via their website, tasting room and at select shops and restaurants in Oregon, Washington, Illinois, and Missouri.

Top restaurants that serve Youngberg Hill Wines

1. Paley's Place, Portland, OR
2. Headwaters, Portland, OR
3. Portland City Gril, Portland, OR
4. The Barberry, McMinnville, OR
5. Tina's, Dundee, OR
6. Michael Smith, Kansas City, MO
7. Charisse's, Kansas City, MO
8. JJs, Kansas City, MO
9. Main Street Social, Libertyville, IL
10. Imperial, Portland, OR

VISITOR INFORMATION

The winery and tasting room can be visited without appointment. Tours and tastings are available at a cost. Group tours (maximum 8 people) are also available. The winery receives about 3,500 visitors annually. The property also includes the 9-room Inn for the perfect retreat, and specializes in exclusive, romantic and personalized weddings and elopement packages.

WINES

Jordan Pinot Noir

Varietals: Pinot Noir (100%)
Barrel Aging: 14 months in French oak; 25% new
Skin Contact: 5 days
Type of Wine: Red
Alcohol: 13,0%
Optimal Serving Temperature: 65° F
Vintage Year: 2015
Bottle Format: 750ml

Bailey Pinot Noir

Varietals: Pinot Noir (100%)
Barrel Aging: 14 months in French oak; 25% new
Skin Contact: 5 days
Type of Wine: Red
Alcohol: 13,0%
Optimal Serving Temperature: 65° F
Vintage Year: 2015
Bottle Format: 750ml
Awards: Double Gold Medal, San Francisco
Chronical International Wine Competition

Aspen Pinot Gris

Varietals: Pinot Gris (100%)
Barrel Aging: Stainless steel
Type of Wine: White
Alcohol: 12,5%
Optimal Serving Temperature: 56° F
Vintage Year: 2017
Bottle Format: 750ml

Natasha Pinot Noir

Varietals: Pinot Noir (100%)
Barrel Aging: 14 months in French oak; 25% new
Skin Contact: 5 days
Type of Wine: Red
Alcohol: 13,0%
Optimal Serving Temperature: 65° F
Vintage Year: 2015
Bottle Format: 750ml

Aspen Chardonnay

Varietals: Chardonnay (100%)
Barrel Aging: 8 months in French oak
Type of Wine: White
Alcohol: 12,5%
Optimal Serving Temperature: 58° F
Vintage Year: 2016
Bottle Format: 750ml

KESWICK VINEYARDS

Keswick, VIRGINIA

www.keswickvineyards.com
E-mail:
tastingroom@keswickvineyards.com
Address: 1575 Keswick Winery Drive,
Keswick, VA 22947
Phone: (434) 244-3341

HISTORY

Keswick Vineyards was established in 2000, when Al Schornberg and his wife Cindy purchased the Edgewood Estate. All vineyards were established from the ground up, and the winery produced it's first commercial vintage in 2002, winning the honor of "Best White Wine in America" at the Atlanta International Wine Summit.

With approximately 45 acres under vine, the focus is on producing small lot, vineyard driven wines that showcase the terroir of the estate. With the backdrop of the majestic Blue Ridge Mountains, visitors are welcome to taste the award winning wines and spend the afternoon taking in the breathtaking views the winery has to offer.

OWNERSHIP & MANAGEMENT

Al and Cindy Schornberg, hailing from Holly Michigan, purchased the Edgewood Estate that is home to Keswick Vineyards in 2002. After an extensive search that spanned coast to coast, they eventually settled in Virginia to realize their dream of owning a winery. After a successful career in the technology industry where Al owned a Fortune 500 company, a near fatal plane accident proved the catalyst for realizing and pursuing their dream. Keswick Vineyards is a family owned and operated winery with three children currently involved with operations. Their winemaker Stephen Barnard is married to Al's second eldest daughter Kath and hails from South Africa where he studied winemaking before coming to the United States.

WINEMAKER

Stephen Barnard studied Viticulture and Enology at Elsenbug Agricultural College in South Africa, and after graduation came to Virginia in 2002 as an intern. His experience includes

stints at the oldest winery in South Africa as well as Morgenhof and Flagstone wineries.

Other than a two year stint at Rappahannock Cellars in Northern Virginia, Stephen has been involved exclusively with Keswick Vineyards. His winemaking style is one of minimalist intervention, choosing to produce wines that reflect the soul of the soil and the expression of the Estate's terroir. His wines are mostly single varietals that require some aging in the bottle, some seeing 10 years quite easily. His mantra is a simple one, these wines are better than last years, but not as good as the next.

VINEYARD
The winery owns 400 acres of land, out of which 42 acres are under vine. The vineyard covers a range of soils that vary in composition from heavy clay to decomposed granite and shist. They have typical albemarle clay in the front portion of the vineyard, which has good water holding capacity planted to Viognier, Verdejo, Touriga and Norton. In the back portion of the vineyards they have decomposed granite and very rocky soil which has excellent drainage and is planted to their premium Bordeaux grapes. It promotes low vigor vines but produces excellent quality grapes which historically produce their best wines.

Some fermentations are inoculated, and their estate Reserve wines are all allowed to ferment naturally. Most of their whites are fermented in temperature controlled tanks, with their Reserve wines receiving no inoculation of yeast. Reds are fermented in both tank and smaller one-ton fermentation bins depending on the lot size.

Keswick wines are available through the tasting room and wine club.

GRAPES GROWN

- Viognier
- Norton
- Cabernet Sauvignon
- Touriga Nacionale
- Cabernet Franc
- Chardonnay
- Merlot
- Petit Verdot
- Chambourcin
- Other

42 ACRES

85 TONNES

Top restaurants that serve Keswick Wines

1. Keswick Hall, Keswick, VA
2. Ivy Inn, Charlottesville, VA
3. Aberdeen Barn, Charlottesville, VA

VISITOR INFORMATION

The winery and tasting room can be visited without appointment. Tastings are available at a cost. The winery receives about 22,000 visitors annually and is also available for private events:

WINES

Cabernet Sauvignon Estate Reserve

Varietals: Cabernet Savignon (100%)
Barrel Aging: 22 months in French and American oak
Skin Contact: 21 days
Type of Wine: Red
Alcohol: 13,8%
Optimal Serving Temperature: 65° F
Vintage Year: 2010
Bottle Format: 750ml
Awards: Gold Medal, 2015 China Wine & Spirits Awards; Gold Medal, 2014 San Francisco International Wine Competition; Gold Medal, 2013 & 2015 Virginia Governor's Cup

Cabernet Franc Estate Reserve

Varietals: Cabernet Franc (100%)
Barrel Aging: 10 months in French and American oak; 33% new
Skin Contact: 14 days
Type of Wine: Red
Alcohol: 14,0%
Optimal Serving Temperature: 58° F
Vintage Year: 2014
Bottle Format: 750ml

Chardonnay Estate Reserve

Varietals: Chardonnay (100%)
Barrel Aging: 10 months in French oak
Type of Wine: White
Alcohol: 14,0%
Optimal Serving Temperature: 55° F
Vintage Year: 2014
Bottle Format: 750ml

Viognier Estate Reserve

Varietals: Viognier (100%)
Barrel Aging: 8 months in French oak
Type of Wine: White
Alcohol: 14,0%
Optimal Serving Temperature: 55° F
Vintage Year: 2014
Bottle Format: 750ml

PEARMUND CELLARS

Broad Run, VIRGINIA

www.pearmundcellars.com
E-mail: info@pearmundcellars.com
Address: 6190 Georgetown Road,
Broad Run, VA 20137
Phone: (540) 347-3475

HISTORY

Pearmund Cellars is located in the beautiful foothills of eastern Fauquier County, Virginia. The 7,500 square foot, geothermal winery is nestled in the 15 acres of Meriwether Vineyards, the oldest vineyard in Virginia. Established in 1976, the vineyard originally hosted nine different grape varieties. Today the winery sticks to Chardonnay on the property, as they are the most successful grapes to grow with respect to this terroir. They also source from the premier vineyards of Virginia that specialize in one particular grape variety. Their Italian-tiled barrel room features Spanish antique-gold light fixtures and unique barrel stacking systems. The perfect setting for an intimate, candlelit "Will you marry me?" catered dinner for two or a team-building off-site corporate meeting. Over the years, owner Chris Pearmund has garnered much attention and accolades for his talent and ability to produce quality wines.

OWNERSHIP & MANAGEMENT

Owner Chris Pearmund is one of Virginia's most widely recognized and well-respected winegrowers and winemakers. Chris has enjoyed careers; the military, marine biology, and sporting goods. But it was working in restaurants that lighted his passion for wine. In 1991 Chris started a mobile bottling business. In 1993 he purchased Meriwether Vineyards and

created Pearmund Cellars. In 1994 he was offering his services as a consultant, working with 40 wineries in 10 different states. Today, Chris is still consulting, and opening wineries, but his namesake winery is his pride and joy: Pearmund Cellars. He has more than 25 years of experience as a Winemaker, Vineyard Manager and Winery Operator. Chris is the "go-to" guy if you want to understand the wine industry from berry to bottle. He has taught and mentored numerous professionals in the industry. A few accomplishments of note include: President of the Virginia Vineyards Association, Chairman of the Virginia Wine and Food Society, 1st mobile wine bottler this side of the Rocky Mountains, 1st winery to use OXO barrel system, which is now the gold standard for barrel rooms, innovator of the barrel ownership program. In addition, his wines have garnered many medals.

In 2012 Chris took a new and enthusiastic winemaker under his wing. Winemaker, J. Ashton Lough, a native Virginian, always had a love for science and art. In high school, he attended the Governor's School for Science and Technology, and then graduated from VMI. He had several occupations before finding winemaking; from training as an oil painter under a famous French impressionist to working as an electrician. Ashton returned to school in 2008. He graduated from the University of Georgia in 2012 with degrees in Biochemistry and Molecular Biology. He then did post graduate work in the University's Department of Biochemistry. It was during this time when he started making wine and researching winemaking, reading most every winemaking text in print. Finding his passion in life, he left the university and began as Winemaker under Executive Winemaker, Chris Pearmund in 2012. He is currently Winemaker at Vint Hill, Pearmund Cellars, and The Winery at Bull Run.

VINEYARD
The winery owns 30 acres of land, and leases another 67 acres, all of which is under vine. They have various vineyards for particular wine types grown. Their estate of Meriwether Vineyard is now 40 years old and recognized as Virginia's oldest vineyard.

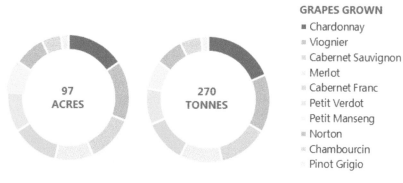

GRAPES GROWN

- Chardonnay
- Viognier
- Cabernet Sauvignon
- Merlot
- Cabernet Franc
- Petit Verdot
- Petit Manseng
- Norton
- Chambourcin
- Pinot Grigio

97 ACRES

270 TONNES

Pearmund wines are sold mainly on site, but also in several wonderful restaurants in the Northern Virginia region. Their local Wegmans market stocks a few of their varietals. Wines are also available via their website.

Top restaurants that serve Pearmund Wines

1. Bonefish Grill, Gainesville, VA
2. The Bridge, Warrenton, VA
3. Poplar Springs, Casanova, VA
4. Inn at Little Washington, Washington, VA
5. Urbana, Washington DC
6. Café Torino, Warrenton VA

VISITOR INFORMATION
The winery and tasting room can be visited without appointment. Tastings and winery tours are available at a cost. The winery receives about 35,000 visitors annually and is also available for private events.

WINES

Ameritage

Varietals: Cabernet Sauvignon (71%), Merlot
(11%), Petit Verdot (9%), Cabernet Franc (8%),
Malbec (1%)
Barrel Aging: 12 months in Virginia oak; 50%
new
Skin Contact: 17 days
Type of Wine: Red
Alcohol: 13,7%
Optimal Serving Temperature: 63° F
Vintage Year: 2013
Bottle Format: 750ml

Viognier

Varietals: Viognier (100%)
Barrel Aging: 10 months in French oak and
acacia
Type of Wine: White
Alcohol: 13,7%
Optimal Serving Temperature: 55° F
Vintage Year: 2013
Bottle Format: 750ml

PHILIP CARTER WINERY

Hume, VIRGINIA

www.pcwinery.com
E-mail: info@pcwinery.com
Address: 4366 Stillhouse Road Hume, VA 22639
Phone: (540) 364-1203

HISTORY
There are few places that can boast the rich depth of American wine history that Philip Carter Winery reflects. The family name carries a 250-year legacy dating back to 1762 as producers of the first internationally recognized fine wines in America. Today, that legacy is being carried forward by Philip Carter Strother. Located in Hume, Virginia, Philip Carter Winery is seated on 27 acres among rolling hills and vineyards in the heart of Fauquier County's Wine Country.

OWNERSHIP & MANAGEMENT
Philip Carter Strother - an attorney who serves as general counsel to many Virginia farm wineries - purchased Stillhouse Vineyards in 2008 and renamed the property to honor his family's early winemaking history. Emmanuel Galineau is a 5th generation winemaker from France. He began making wine at the age of 13 on his family's vineyard and went on to earn Bachelor's and Master's degrees in Viticulture and Enology. Emmanuel grew up on his family farm where he learned most of what he knows today. He has worked in Chile, California, Washington, Switzerland, Portugal and France.

VINEYARD
The winery owns 27 acres, out of which 11 acres are under vine. Bedrock is very close to the surface and makes a low fertility. The soil is composed of a lot of clay. They mostly use commercial yeast to ferment the grapes. Their fermentation process is very basic. They co-inoculate before alcoholic fermentation. For red wines, maceration is extended with good structure. For whites, partial alcoholic fermentation is done in barrels.

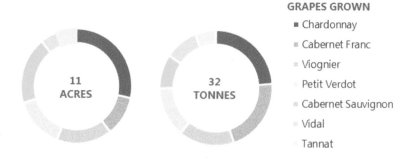

11 ACRES

32 TONNES

GRAPES GROWN
- Chardonnay
- Cabernet Franc
- Viognier
- Petit Verdot
- Cabernet Sauvignon
- Vidal
- Tannat

Philip Carter wines are available in select Virginia ABC stores.

VISITOR INFORMATION

The winery and tasting room can be visited without appointment. Best seasons to visit are Spring and Summer. Winery tours and tastings are available at a cost. Group tours (maximum 10 people) are available. The winery receives about 14,000 visitors annually and is also available for private events:

WINES

Cleve

Varietals: Petit Verdot (50%), Tannat (50%)
Barrel Aging: 20 months in French oak; 20% new
Skin Contact: 15-20 days
Type of Wine: Red
Alcohol: 13,5%
Optimal Serving Temperature: 63° F
Vintage Year: 2010
Bottle Format: 750ml
Awards: Gold Medal, 2013 Virginia Governor's Cup

Rosé

Varietals: Merlot (100%)
Skin Contact: 24 hours
Type of Wine: Rosé
Alcohol: 12,0%
Optimal Serving Temperature: 52° F
Vintage Year: 2014
Bottle Format: 750ml

Corotoman

Varietals: Cabernet Sauvignon (40%), Merlot (35%), Cabernet Franc (25%)
Barrel Aging: 20 months in French oak; 20% new
Skin Contact: 15-20 days
Type of Wine: Red
Alcohol: 13,0%
Optimal Serving Temperature: 63° F
Vintage Year: 2012
Bottle Format: 750ml
Awards: Silver Medal, 2015 Virginia Governor's Cup

Meritage

Varietals: Cabernet Franc (42%) , Petit Verdot (32%), Cabernet Sauvignon (21%), Merlot (5%)
Barrel Aging: 18 months in French oak
Skin Contact: 15-20 days
Type of Wine: Red
Alcohol: 13,0%
Optimal Serving Temperature: 63° F
Vintage Year: 2010
Bottle Format: 750ml
Awards: Gold Medal, 2014 San Francisco International Wine Competition; Bronze Medal, 2012 Atlantic Seaboard Competition

BRIAN CARTER CELLARS

Woodinville, WASHINGTON

www.briancartercellars.com
E-mail: info@briancartercellars.com
Address: 14419 Woodinville Redmond Road NE, Woodinville, WA 98072
Phone: (425) 806-9463

HISTORY

Since Brian Carter's arrival on the Washington State wine scene in 1980 when there were just 16 wineries, Brian continues to influence this industry which now boasts more than 900 wineries and is growing weekly. His involvement as winemaker, consultant, and guide to dozens of wineries has helped elevate the Washington wine industry from a regional industry to an international powerhouse.

Brian Carter's initial success laid the foundation for his steady ascent. In 1997, after years of producing wines for others, Brian created a small production of his own wine, "Solesce," at the Apex Winery where he was residing as winemaker and co-owner. The wine quickly sold out and the time for Brian Carter Cellars had arrived. With the introduction of the Brian Carter Cellars Collection, Brian completed one aspect of his outstanding career and began another. In 2006, Brian released his full line of blended wines, including Oriana, Tuttorosso, Byzance, and Le Coursier (formerly L'Etalon). Brian Carter Cellars became the first winery in Washington dedicated exclusively to producing blends.

Brian's passion for winemaking has always been his hallmark, and his European-style blended wines are the culmination of his years as a premier Washington winemaker. With his connections to the best vineyards in the state, he is able to source the finest quality grapes to achieve his vision of wines with balance, dimension, and depth. The Brian Carter Cellars epitomizes Brian's commitment to quality, taste and terroir.

OWNERSHIP & MANAGEMENT

Brian's early curiosity about microbes led him to study Microbiology at Oregon State University where he discovered his appreciation for the wines of Oregon. After two years at the University of California, Davis, Brian honed his winemaking skill with stints at esteemed California wineries Mount Eden Vineyard and Chateau Montelena. But the Pacific Northwest beckoned, and Brian returned to join early Washington winemaker Paul Thomas Winery, where his skills and artistic touch marked him as a winemaker to watch. At a competition held at Windows on the World in New York City, Brian's 1983 Paul Thomas Cabernet took first place, outpacing the likes of Quilceda Creek and Chateau Lafite-Rothschild.

Brian was twice touted as "Winemaker of the Year" by Washington Magazine, and he is the only three-time recipient of the Pacific Northwest Enological Society's Grand Prize. Often recognized by his peers, Brian was the Honored Vintner at the 2007 Auction of Washington Wines, and he received the prestigious Industry Service Award from the Washington Association of Wine Grape Growers. Dedicated to giving back to the industry that has supported him, Brian is a long-standing member and past chairman of the Wine Research Advisory Committee which makes recommendations on how state funds are spent on wine and grape research at Washington State University.

VINEYARD

Brian Carter Cellars purchases grapes from a number of different vineyards around Washington. The eleven most important vineyards from which they source their grapes from are Klipsun Vineyard and E & E Shaw Vineyards within the Red Mountain AVA, Stone Tree Vineyard within the Wahluke Slope, Lonesome Spring Ranch, Olsen Vineyards and Chandler Reach Vineyards within the Yakima Valley AVA, Solstice Vineyard located high on the Rosa north of Prosser, Upland Vineyards within the Snipes Mountain AVA, Stillwater Creek Vineyard within the Columbia Valley AVA and Dineen Vineyards within the Rattlesnake Hills AVA.

Brian Carter Cellars wines are available at their tasting room and at restaurants, wine shops and retail locations throughout Washington, Oregon, Idaho and Northern Nevada. The wines are also exported to China.

Top restaurants that serve Brian Carter Cellars Wines

1. Daniel's Broiler, four locations throughout the Puget Sound, WA
2. Grazie Café Italiano, Canyon Park, WA
3. Place Pigalle, Seattle, WA
4. Tandem Wine & Cheese Bar, Woodinville, WA
5. Purple Café, Seattle and Woodinville, WA
6. Blueacre Seafood, Seattle, WA
7. Pearl Restaurant, Bellevue, WA
8. Cask and Schooner, Seattle WA
9. Laguna Café, Seattle, WA
10. Steelhead Diner, Seattle WA

VISITOR INFORMATION
The winery and tasting room can be visited without appointment. Tastings are available at a cost. The winery receives about 3,000 visitors annually.

WINES

Solesce

Varietals: Cabernet Sauvignon (54%), Merlot (25%), Petit Verdot (9%), Cabernet Franc (7%), Malbec (5%)
Barrel aging: 30 months in French oak; 50% new
Type of Wine: Red
Alcohol: 14,2%
Vintage Year: 2013
Bottle Format: 750ml
Awards: Double Gold Medal, 2018 Tri-Cities Wine Festival

Opulento

Varietals: Tourigan Nacional (58%), Souzao (21%), Tinta Roriz (11%), Tinta Cao (10%)
Barrel aging: 22 months in French oak; 15% new
Type of Wine: Dessert
Alcohol: 19,0%
Vintage Year: 2013
Bottle Format: 375ml
Awards: Gold Medal, 2015 Jefferson Cup Invitational Wine Competition

Trentenaire

Varietals: Petit Verdot (62%), Merlot (18%), Cabernet Sauvignon (10%), Malbec (5%), Cabernet Franc (5%)
Barrel aging: 22 months in French oak; 40% new
Type of Wine: Red
Alcohol: 14,1%
Vintage Year: 2013
Bottle Format: 750ml
Awards: Double Platinum Medal, 2017 Wine Press Northwest

Oriana

Varietals: Viognier (50%), Roussanne (40%), Riesling (10%)
Barrel aging: 1/3 in French oak; 2/3 in stainless steel
Type of Wine: White
Alcohol: 13,6%
Vintage Year: 2017
Bottle Format: 750ml
Awards: Silver Medal, 2018 Jefferson Cup Invitational Wine Competition

Corrida

Varietals: Tempranillo (66%), Graciano (18%), Cabernet Sauvignon (10%), Garnacha (6%)
Barrel aging: 22 months in French, Russian and American oak; 30% new
Type of Wine: Red
Alcohol: 14,1%
Vintage Year: 2014
Bottle Format: 750ml
Awards: Silver Medal, 2018 Seattle Wine Awards

Le Coursier

Varietals: Merlot (54%), Cabernet Sauvignon (22%), Cabernet Franc (14%), Malbec (6%), Petit Verdot (4%)
Barrel aging: 22 months in French oak; 40% new
Type of Wine: Red
Alcohol: 14,0%
Vintage Year: 2013
Bottle Format: 750ml
Awards: Double Gold Medal, 2018 Seattle Wine Awards

Byzance

Varietals: Grenache (53%), Syrah (22%), Mourvédre (17%), Counoise (5%), Cinsault (3%)
Barrel aging: 22 months in French oak; 20% new
Type of Wine: Red
Alcohol: 14,2%
Vintage Year: 2013
Bottle Format: 750ml
Awards: Double Gold Medal, 2017 Seattle Wine Awards

Takahashi

Varietals: Malbec (58%), Merlot (34%), Cabernet Franc (8%)
Barrel aging: French oak; 35% new
Type of Wine: Red
Alcohol: 14,0%
Vintage Year: 2015
Bottle Format: 750ml
Awards: Gold Medal, 2018 Washington State Wine Awards

Tuttorosso

Varietals: Sangiovese (68%), Cabernet Sauvignon (18%), Syrah (14%)
Barrel aging: 24 months in French and European oak; 20% new
Type of Wine: Red
Alcohol: 14,3%
Vintage Year: 2014
Bottle Format: 750ml
Awards: Silver Medal, 2018 Tri-Cities Wine Festival

Brian Carter Cellars Photos by Richard Duval

CAIRDEAS WINERY

Manson, WASHINGTON

www.cairdeaswinery.com
E-mail: info@cairdeaswinery.com
Address: 31 Winesap Avenue, Manson, WA 98831
Phone: (509) 687-0555

HISTORY

Charlie and Lacey Lybecker pull their winemaking inspiration from southern France, crafting traditional and truly unique blends featuring Washington-grown Rhône varietals. Cairdeas (pronounced 'Card-iss'), a nod to their heritage, is an Irish Gaelic word meaning friendship, goodwill or alliance.

Cairdeas Winery was founded in West Seattle in 2009. In 2012, the Lybeckers moved their winery and family to the Lake Chelan Valley in north central Washington. They desired to be part of a youthful and growing wine region, establishing their own roots in the AVA with the planting of their estate vineyard in 2015.

OWNERSHIP & MANAGEMENT

Charlie & Lacey Lybecker built Cairdeas Winery from the ground up, establishing their winemaking foundation while maintaining full time careers in website development for the radio industry and marketing in the event and hospitality industry, respectively. The production of 250 cases in their first vintage increased to 4,000 cases in their tenth vintage.

Charlie is the Winemaker at Cairdeas. His curiosity for what makes the wines turn out the way that they do (vineyards, barrels, yeast, wine making techniques) ignites his passion to discover how truly great wines are made. He has always been fascinated with wines from the Rhône Valley of France which is reflected in their vineyard choices and in the wines that they make.

Along with helping in the cellar at harvest, bottling, working the tasting bar, sweeping the floors, and washing the glassware, Lacey is the guru behind all of the marketing and promotions that it takes to keep Cairdeas Winery going.

VINEYARD

The winery covers 6 acres of land, out of which 2 acres are under vine. In addition, they also source grapes from several different vineyards. Their estate sits on a south facing slope on the north shore of Lake Chelan, Washington. Due to the ice age glaciers that formed Lake Chelan, the soil surrounding the lake has distinctive properties such as coarse, sandy sediment with notable amounts of quartz and mica.

For some of their wines they use cultured yeasts that were isolated out of vineyards in France. For other wines they bring the fruit in from the vineyard and let the natural yeast from the vineyard ferment the wines. They try to do cooler and longer fermentations. This allows them to get good color without over-extracting bitter tannins. Wines are processed very gently, fermentation takes place while grapes are still attached to the stems.

2 ACRES

6 TONNES

GRAPES GROWN

- Syrah
- Clairette Blanche
- Picardan

Cairdeas wines are available in their tasting room, via their website and in select wine shops, grocery stores and restaurants within the state of Washington.

Top restaurants that serve Cairdeas Wines

1. Visconti's, Wenatchee, WA
2. Riverwalk Inn & Café, Chelan, WA
3. Andante, Chelan, WA
4. Arrowleaf Bistro, Winthrop, WA
5. Sun Mountain Lodge, Winthrop, WA
6. Picolino's, Seattle, WA
7. North Shore Café, Manson, WA
8. Freestone Inn, Mazama, WA
9. Reds Wine Bar, Kent, WA
10. Campbell's Resort, Chelan, WA

VISITOR INFORMATION
The winery and tasting room can be visited without appointment. Tours and tastings are available at a cost. Group tours (maximum 15 people) are also available. The winery receives about 10,000 visitors annually.

WINES

Tri

Varietals: Syrah (73%), Mourvèdre (16%), Grenache (11%)
Barrel Aging: 18 months in French oak; 30% new
Skin Contact: 17 days
Type of Wine: Red
Alcohol: 14,0%
Optimal Serving Temperature: 68 ˚F
Vintage Year: 2016
Bottle Format: 750ml

Consonance

Varietals: Petite Sirah (50%), Syrah (45%), Viognier (5%)
Barrel Aging: 18 months in French oak; 50% new
Skin Contact: 17 days
Type of Wine: Red
Alcohol: 14,7%
Optimal Serving Temperature: 68 ˚F
Vintage Year: 2016
Bottle Format: 750ml

Nellie Mae

Varietals: Viognier (65%), Roussanne (35%)
Barrel Aging: Stainless steel
Type of Wine: White
Alcohol: 12,8%
Optimal Serving Temperature: 48 ˚F
Vintage Year: 2018
Bottle Format: 750ml

Cinsault

Varietals: Cinsault (75%), Alicante Bouschet (25%)
Barrel Aging: 18 months in French oak; 20% new
Skin Contact: 17 days
Type of Wine: Red
Alcohol: 14,0%
Optimal Serving Temperature: 68 ˚F
Vintage Year: 2016
Bottle Format: 750ml

Caislén an Papa

Varietals: Grenache (37%), Mourvèdre (26%), Syrah (16%), Counoise (11%), Cinsault (10%)
Barrel Aging: 18 months in French oak
Skin Contact: 17 days
Type of Wine: Red
Alcohol: 14,0%
Optimal Serving Temperature: 68 ˚F
Vintage Year: 2016
Bottle Format: 750ml

Cairdeas Winery Photos by DalisaJo Photography and Oly Mingo

CAVE B ESTATE WINERY

Quincy, WASHINGTON

www.caveb.com
E-mail: events@caveb.com
Address: 348 Silica Road, Quincy, WA 98848
Phone: (509) 785-3500

HISTORY

Vince Bryan was born in Brooklyn, New York, living next door to his Italian grandparents and soaking up the Italian culture. He loved the energy of the city but sometimes would look out his window onto the alley below and dream of open spaces and farming. Eventually he moved to the suburbs outside of Chicago and met his beautiful wife & life partner, Carol Bryan. He would go on to become a Neurosurgeon and move with Carol and their 4 children to Washington State. In 1980 they purchased a several-hundred acre parcel of land high on the cliffs above the Columbia River. The closest town was Quincy and at the time the nearest paved road was interstate 90, six miles away. The Bryans had been on a year-long quest to find land in Washington State which was similar in latitude to the great wine-growing regions of France, and which had both the soils and microclimates needed to grow premium grapes.

When Vince and Carol Bryan chose this land for their vineyards, they immediately saw that they had also received much more than they bargained for. They were now in possession of a piece of land which was extraordinary in its natural drama and beauty. To have such amazing conditions for the growing of premium wine grapes, coupled with a location so stunning in its sweeping, panoramic gorge cliffs, valleys and views, was extraordinary. By 1984 their first winery Champs de Brionne opened. After 7 years of growth they sold the winery to return their focus to growing premium grapes, which they did for the next 10 years. In 2000 they decided to start their 2nd winery, a smaller, premium winery, focusing on food friendly wines and unique events to bring people together. By 2005 they built a destination resort with 55 rooms, a spa, pool and restaurant which they sold after 12 years of bountiful growth. They retained the vineyards, winery and developing properties which they began to build out into the Cave B Ridge Condos in 2017.

Today, Cave B Estate Winery is an award winning winery, known for its large variety of consistent high-quality wines made from 100% estate vines. The Bryans launched an outdoor theater in 2017, Stage B. Stage B is located directly in front of their Quincy tasting room with views of the estate vineyards below, allowing guests to enjoy the perfect pairing of music and wine.

OWNERSHIP & MANAGEMENT

Cave B Estate Winery is owned and founded by Vince and Carol Bryan. Their daughter Carrie is in charge of branding, marketing & events for both the winery and Stage B, their summer music theater. Carrie's husband, Freddy Arredondo, whom she met on a professional cooking program in Italy, but who was born and raised in southern California, changed careers from a professional chef to a professional winemaker after spending more time at his in-laws vineyards and falling in love with the vines and wine. Freddy started

realizing he was reading more about wine and winemaking then about food and cooking and knew he wanted to go back to school to pursue a degree in Enology and Viticulture while taking everything he had learned from his cooking career into his new pursuit. After 2 years of schooling, internships and working as an Assistant Winemaker, Freddy became the Head Winemaker of Cave B Estate Winery in 2008. He is also the General Manager of the Quincy Tasting room. Janet Bryan, daughter-in law to Vince and Carol serves as the Chief Financial Officer of the winery and oversees the management at their Woodinville tasting room.

VINEYARD
The Bryans own 430 acres of land, out of which 100 acres are under vine. Their Cave B Vineyards also known as Familigia Vineyards surrounds Cave B Estate Winery creating ideal harvesting conditions for their Winemaker as well as a gorgeous setting for their tasting room. It's a part of the Ancient Lakes of the Columbia Valley AVA in Washington State.

They grow 17 varieties of grapes and have a unique property with many mini-microclimates, and have a combination of shallow, well drained sandy to silt loam soils, with a combination of rocks ranging from pomace basalt to solid basalt and Calcium Carbonate in crusted stones with solid chunks of limestone within the soil profile.

Reds are fermented in small lot, open-top bins with manual punch-downs during the fermentation. They are fermented at cool temperatures, that do not exceed 80° F. Whites are fermented predominantly in stainless steel tanks. They are also fermented at cool temperatures, but the whites do not exceed 55° F. The white wines remain on the lees until they are bottled to enhance structure and mouthfeel.

GRAPES GROWN

- Chardonnay
- Cabernet Sauvignon
- Riesling
- Malbec
- Merlot
- Sauvignon Blanc
- Syrah
- Tempranillo
- Cabernet Franc
- Other

100 ACRES

383 TONNES

Cave B wines are available in both their Quincy and Woodinville tasting rooms, with a third tasting room opening in Tri-cities, Washington in 2019 as well as through their website, large wine club and in select retail outlets and restaurants.

VISITOR INFORMATION
The winery and tasting rooms can be visited without appointment. Tastings are available at a cost. The winery receives about 10,000 visitors annually and is also available for private events.

WINES

Cuvee Du Soleil

Varietals: Cabernet Sauvignon (42%), Merlot (34%), Cabernet Franc (8%), Malbec (8%), Petit Verdot (8%)
Barrel Aging: 22 months in French and American oak
Skin Contact: 20 days
Type of Wine: Red
Alcohol: 14,7%
Optimal Serving Temperature: 62 °F
Vintage Year: 2015
Bottle Format: 750ml

Malbec

Varietals: Malbec (100%)
Barrel Aging: 22 months in French and American oak
Skin Contact: 20 days
Type of Wine: Red
Alcohol: 14,3%
Optimal Serving Temperature: 62 °F
Vintage Year: 2016
Bottle Format: 750ml

Chenin Blanc

Varietals: Chenin Blanc (100%)
Type of Wine: White
Alcohol: 13,1%
Optimal Serving Temperature: 44 °F
Vintage Year: 2018
Bottle Format: 750ml

Roussanne

Varietals: Roussanne (90%), Viognier (10%)
Barrel Aging: 10 months in French oak; 10% new
Type of Wine: White
Alcohol: 13,9%
Optimal Serving Temperature: 44 °F
Vintage Year: 2018
Bottle Format: 750ml

DELILLE CELLARS

Woodinville, WASHINGTON

www.delillecellars.com
E-mail: contact@delillecellars.com
Address: 14421 Woodinville-Redmond
Road NE, Woodinville 98072; 15 Lake
Street, Kirkland 98033
Phone: (425) 489-0544

HISTORY

DeLille Cellars is a boutique artisan winery located in Woodinville, Washington. Founded in 1992 and currently the third oldest winery in Woodinville, DeLille Cellars pioneered Bordeaux-style blends in Washington State. DeLille Cellars is considered a principal influence in establishing Washington as a premier region for viticulture with a strong tradition of quality and excellence over its 27-year history. Today, the winery has a portfolio of over a dozen Bordeaux and Rhône style blends true to the terroir of Washington State.

The winery's passion lies in showcasing the powerful, concentrated and structured fruit of Washington State through the European art of blending - not only through various combinations of Bordeaux and Rhône grape varieties, but also via combining fruit from acclaimed vineyards to express the unique terroir of the region. DeLille Cellars focuses on the Red Mountain AVA and grape sourcing from Washington's leading Grand Cru vineyards.

OWNERSHIP & MANAGEMENT

The winery was founded in 1992 by Charles and Greg Lill, Jay Soloff and celebrated winemaker Chris Upchurch. Chris' love for wine started in his youth, with extensive travel throughout the Grand Cru wine-growing regions of Europe and the west coast of the United States. After graduating with a Bachelor of Science degree from the University of Washington, Chris began his career as a wine merchant, working with several of Seattle's best-known restaurants. This experience allowed him to hone his palate while tasting wines from around the world. Deep in his heart, Chris knew he wanted to express his passion in the production end of the wine industry.

Armed with his love of wine and commitment to learning its craft, Chris initially developed a successful grape-brokerage business contracting grapes from Washington State and selling them to winemakers. Chris uncovered his true calling once he started spending endless hours in the vineyards. That love of the land, the vine and its fruit, fostered Chris' passion of winemaking and his passion for charting a course in Washington State. An

acclaimed professional winemaker for over twenty years, Chris still spends much of his time in the vineyards of Washington State, primarily Yakima Valley and Red Mountain AVA's.

WINEMAKER

Jason Gorski, Director of Winemaking for DeLille Cellars, found his passion for wine while studying biology at Duke University where he was introduced to a respected sommelier by his academic advisor. This experience guided Jason to Washington State in 2004, where he worked at the state's founding winery, Chateau Ste. Michelle, in Woodinville, Washington. Jason was then offered the role of Assistant Winemaker at Spring Valley Vineyard in Walla Walla, Washington. Jason joined DeLille Cellars in 2011 as Assistant Winemaker, where, under the tutelage of Founding Winemaker Chris Upchurch, he ultimately became Winemaker in 2014 and in January of 2019 was promoted to Director of Winemaking. Jason has been instrumental in the growth of DeLille Cellars while maintaining the winery's tradition of quality and excellence.

VINEYARD

DeLille Cellars has a sterling reputation for sourcing fruit from the oldest and most respected vineyards in Washington State, with a focus on the acclaimed Red Mountain AVA. Key vineyards include Ciel du Cheval, Upchurch, Boushey, Harrison Hill, Red Willow, Klipsun, Quintessence and the winery's estate vineyard on Red Mountain, Grand Ciel.

The Red Mountain AVA is the smallest, warmest wine-grape growing region in Washington. It has a unique combination of diverse geology, gentle south slope, consistent winds and a notable heat profile. A complex mixture of the most rare and highly valued soil types in Washington was created by wind-blown silt and sand over glacial outflow.

DeLille uses a combination of native fermentation and commercially available cultured yeast, dependent upon the vineyard block and program. In general, white grapes are whole-cluster pressed and cold settled before fermented slowly at cool temperatures. Red grapes are destemmed and spend an average of 12 to 16 days on skins, with select lots extended macerated for 60 or more days. DeLille's fermentation philosophy is minimalist, with nutrient additions only when necessary.

556 TONNES

GRAPES GROWN

- Merlot
- Cabernet Sauvignon
- Sauvignon Blanc
- Syrah
- Semillon
- Petit Verdot
- Cabernet Franc
- Mourvedre
- Grenache
- Other

DeLille wines are available at their website, tasting rooms and are distributed to over 40 states in the United States. The wines are exported to Europe, Canada, Mexico, China, Japan, South Korea and the Phillipines.

Top restaurants that serve DeLille Wines

1. Four Seasons Hotels, various locations across the United States
2. Flemings, various locations across the United States
3. Omni Hotels, various locations across the United States
4. Ritz-Carlton, various locations across the United States
5. Morton's, various locations across the United States
6. Ruth's Chris, various locations across the United States
7. Capital Grille, Seattle, WA
8. Del Frisco's, various locations across the United States
9. BLT Steak/BLT Prime, various locations across the United States
10. Eleven Madison Park, New York, NY

VISITOR INFORMATION
The winery and tasting rooms can be visited without appointment. Tastings are available at a cost.

WINES

D2

Varietals: Merlot (59%), Cabernet Sauvignon (34%), Cabernet Franc (4%), Malbec (2%), Petit Verdot (1%)
Type of Wine: Red
Vintage Year: 2016
Bottle Format: 750ml

Four Flags

Varietals: Cabernet Sauvignon (100%)
Type of Wine: Red
Vintage Year: 2015
Bottle Format: 750ml
Awards: Best of Class, 2018 Seattle Wine Awards

Chaleur Blanc

Varietals: Sauvignon Blanc (68%); Semillon (32%)
Type of Wine: White
Vintage Year: 2016
Bottle Format: 750ml

Chaleur Estate

Varietals: Cabernet Sauvignon (64%), Merlot (24%), Cabernet Franc (10%), Petit Verdot (2%)
Type of Wine: Red
Vintage Year: 2016
Bottle Format: 750ml

Doyenne

Varietals: Syrah (60%), Cabernet Sauvignon (40%)
Type of Wine: Red
Vintage Year: 2015
Bottle Format: 750ml

Grand Ciel

Varietals: Cabernet Sauvignon (100%)
Type of Wine: Red
Vintage Year: 2015
Bottle Format: 750ml

EIGHT BELLS WINERY

Seattle, WASHINGTON

www.8bellswinery.com
E-mail: contact@8bellswinery.com
Address: 6213B Roosevelt Way NE, Seattle, WA 98115
Phone: (206) 909-6812

HISTORY

Eight Bells Winery was founded by Tim Bates, Andy Shepherd and Frank Michiels in 2009. They began their path in the wine world as amateur winemakers in their garages. Tim started making wine in 1980 with Andy joining in 1993. Frank joined the team in 2006 when he volunteered to help with crush.

To their friends and the local winemaking community they were known as the Shellback Vintners, a Shellback being a sailor who has crossed the equator on a ship. Tim and Andy spent their careers working in Oceanography and part of that time sailing on research ships. They were both Shellbacks and wanted a nautical feel to the winery. Frank's lineage came through his father who was a Shellback from his Navy days sailing on the USS South Dakota in World War II. The triumvirate was born and moved from their garages to a commercial space in the Roosevelt district of Seattle in the summer of 2009. Though the name Shellback could not be used commercially they decided on Eight Bells Winery. Eight Bells referring to the end of a sailor's watch at sea.

OWNERSHIP & MANAGEMENT

All the partners at Eight Bells bring a multitude of managerial skills from their successful careers outside of viticulture and enology. Tim Bates, after receiving his PhD from the University of Washington, began a long and distinguished career in research as an Atmospheric Chemist with the National Oceanic and Oceanographic Administration. During his time with NOAA Tim formed a team of scientists and technicians to gather environmental data from the oceans and led cruises consisting of numerous and varied scientific disciplines. After leaving NOAA Tim took a part-time position at the University of

Washington which allowed him more free time to bring his technical and managerial skills to Eight Bells.

Wine has always been a part of Frank Michiels's life. From his parents owning a liquor and wine store in Hollywood to spending time with family friends in the Napa Valley he's been steeped in the wine industry for the majority of his life. After graduating from Stanford University, Frank started a company exporting wood products to Japan where he lived for years before returning to Washington to attend law school. Since his retirement he has served on several charity boards with a deep commitment to giving while never losing his deep love of wine.

Andy Shepherd's profession was also in the oceanographic community. After college he took a position with NOAA developing the first generation of scientific buoys that would telemeter, in real time, environmental data back from the world's oceans. As the technology developed and the satellites became more advanced it allowed the buoy systems to expand worldwide. Over the years as the program grew and his responsibilities moved into management, his interest in wine grew to the next level. While serving as the Chief Scientist aboard a French research vessel and having wine with meals Andy became a convert.

After 10 years of success, Eight Bells moved to another level with the addition of two new partners, Neal and Denise Ratti. Neal has spent the last 3 decades flying as a captain for a major airline in Seattle. Though he still works full time for the airline, all of his spare time is committed to the winery barrel program, the nuances of blending trials and sales. Denise spent her career working for a major law firm in Seattle until last year when she changed careers. She now spends her time with clients and running the new tasting room.

VINEYARD

Eight Bells Winery's main source of fruit is Red Willow Vineyard, located at the western end of the Yakima Valley. It is one of the oldest and most acclaimed vineyards in the state. Eight Bells Winery is very fortunate to have specific blocks within Red Willow Vineyard. Eight Bells wines are not only designated single vineyard, but most of their wines are tied to a specific block within Red Willow from which they receive all of the fruit of that block. This allows the wines to reflect the distinctive terroir of these blocks every year.

Boushey Vineyards are also some of the oldest and most successful vineyards in Washington. In addition to being the source of their Chardonnay, Eight Bells also sources a selection of Rhône varietals from these vineyards.

At the winery they hand sort the grapes to ensure that only good clusters are used in the fermentation process. They inoculate the crushed red grapes the following day with yeast chosen to bring out the varietal characteristics of the grapes. The fermentation generally lasts 7 to 10 days for the red grapes. Twice a day they punch down and also pulse air into the must to keep the yeast healthy and happy. At the end of fermentation, when most of the sugars are converted to alcohol, they pump the free run juice into barrels. The remaining must is transferred to a membrane press to gently extract the remaining juice. Malolactic bacteria are added to barrels for the secondary fermentation. The barrels are kept warm during this period to keep the bacteria working. Secondary fermentation lasts weeks to months. Once secondary fermentation is finished potassium metabisulfite is added to the wine, and the barrel is moved to the barrel room at 55° F for the wine to age. The barrels are sampled and topped monthly. After a year, they begin experimenting with different blends of wine from the various barrels and grape varieties. When they find the best combination, they blend the wines and return them to the barrels for additional aging.

Eight Bells wines are available at their tasting room and at selected restaurants in the Seattle area.

VISITOR INFORMATION

The winery and tasting room can be visited with prior appointment. Tours and tastings are available at a cost. Group tours (maximum 10 people) are also available. The winery receives over 2,000 visitors annually, and is also available for private events.

WINES

David's Block

Varietals: Cabernet Sauvignon (60%), Malbec (22%), Merlot (7%), Cabernet Franc (5%), Petit Verdot (3%), Carmenere (3%)
Barrel aging: 18 months in new French oak
Skin Contact: 7 days
Type of Wine: Red
Alcohol: 14,5%
Optimal Serving Temperature: 63° F
Vintage Year: 2014
Bottle Format: 750ml

Syrah

Varietals: Syrah (94%), Viognier (4%), Grenache (2%)
Barrel aging: 16 months in oak; 50% new
Skin Contact: 7 days
Type of Wine: Red
Alcohol: 13,9%
Optimal Serving Temperature: 63° F
Vintage Year: 2015
Bottle Format: 750ml

Chardonnay

Varietals: Chardonnay (100%)
Type of Wine: White
Alcohol: 14,1%
Optimal Serving Temperature: 63° F
Vintage Year: 2017
Bottle Format: 750ml

Old Salt

Varietals: Sangiovese (68%), Cabernet Sauvignon (18%), Malbec (9%), Merlot (3%), Cabernet Franc (1%), Petit Verdot (1%)
Barrel aging: 16 months in oak
Skin Contact: 7 days
Type of Wine: Red
Alcohol: 14,5%
Optimal Serving Temperature: 63° F
Vintage Year: 2015
Bottle Format: 750ml

Sangiovese

Varietals: Sangiovese (100%)
Barrel aging: 10 months in oak
Skin Contact: 7 days
Type of Wine: Red
Alcohol: 14,2%
Optimal Serving Temperature: 63° F
Vintage Year: 2016
Bottle Format: 750ml

Eight Bells Winery Photos by Mike Sauer & Frank Michiels

LATAH CREEK WINE CELLARS

Spokane, WASHINGTON

www.latahcreek.com
E-mail: info@latahcreek.com
Address: 13030 E Indiana Avenue,
Spokane, WA 99216
Phone: (509) 926-0164

HISTORY

Latah Creek Wine Cellars, established in 1982 by Mike and Ellena Conway, is a pioneer in Washington State's emerging wine scene. Today only a handful of wineries can boast beginnings dating back to the early 1980s, and fewer still can match the consistency and quality produced by Latah Creek for over 37 years. This family-owned winery continues to blaze new trails in winemaking, producing new varieties each season along with their acclaimed lineup of established wines. Mike and Ellena's focus has been in making wines with natural balance and complexity; ones that not only provide the perfect compliment to a meal, but also give absolute enjoyment by themselves. They accomplish this through the use of traditional, old-world winemaking principles and the selection of extraordinary fruit. Their award-winning history is a testament to their success. Mike and Ellena believe that exceptional wine should be available for all to enjoy daily, a philosophy that is reflected in their moderate wine pricing.

OWNERSHIP & MANAGEMENT

Bringing a continuity that only a second generation can, Mike and Ellena's only child, Natalie, joined the team in 2005. Mike learned his winemaking techniques hands-on rather than at school, therefore, he took an apprenticeship approach to train Natalie in the family trade. Confident in her growing winemaking abilities, Mike collaborated with Natalie on Latah Creek's first dessert red, Natalie's Nectar. Natalie's fresh eyes and forward thinking have brought about a few changes at Latah Creek, including the launch of their Monarch Reserve Reds Series, a small-lot, reserve-quality red wine program. Introduced in 2010, this reserve program allows Natalie to intimately know the grape and the reserve wine showcased.

VINEYARD

They contract grapes from different vineyards in Washington. The soil of most of the vineyards has a sandy loam composition.

32 ACRES

171 TONNES

GRAPES SOURCED

- Riesling
- Pinot Grigio
- Chardonnay
- Merlot
- Malbec
- Muscat

In their fermentation process they use commercially available yeast. 70% of Latah Creek's production is white wine. A temperature-controlled fermentation is carried on at between 45 and 50° F for most light and fruity wines. Virtually all fermentations are stopped by refrigeration leaving wines naturally sweet. The only exception would be Chardonnay and possibly Pinot Gris depending upon the year.

Latah Creek wines are primarily available in their tasting room, in the state of Washington with retail outlets also in Northern Oregon, Northern Idaho, and Montana.

VISITOR INFORMATION

The winery and tasting room can be visited without appointment. Tours and tastings are available at a cost. Group tours (maximum 40 people) are also available. The winery receives about 15,000 visitors annually, and is also available for private events.

WINES

Mike's Reserve Red - Columbia Valley

Varietals: Temranillo (48%), Merlot (35%), Zinfandel (9%), Cabernet Sauvignon (8%)
Barrel Aging: 8-24 months in oak
Skin Contact: 14-18 days
Type of Wine: Red
Alcohol: 13,5%
Optimal Serving Temperature: 63 °F
Bottle Format: 750ml

Pinot Gris - Yakima Valley

Varietals: Pinot Gris (100%)
Barrel Aging: Stainless steel
Type of Wine: White
Alcohol: 12,0%
Optimal Serving Temperature: 50 °F
Vintage Year: 2017
Bottle Format: 750ml

Moscato - Yakima Valley

Varietals: Orange Muscat (100%)
Barrel aging: Stainless steel
Type of Wine: White
Alcohol: 6,0%
Optimal Serving Temperature: 40 °F
Vintage Year: 2018
Bottle Format: 750ml

Riesling - Ancient Lakes

Varietals: Riesling (100%)
Barrel Aging: Stainless steel
Type of Wine: White
Alcohol: 10,5%
Optimal Serving Temperature: 50 °F
Vintage Year: 2017
Bottle Format: 750ml

Malbec – Ancient Lakes

Varietals: Malbec (100%)
Barrel Aging: 8 months in oak
Skin Contact: 16 days
Type of Wine: Red
Alcohol: 12,5%
Optimal Serving Temperature: 63 °F
Vintage Year: 2018
Bottle Format: 750ml

MAISON BLEUE WINERY

Walla Walla, WASHINGTON

www.maisonbleuewinery.com
E-mail: info@mbwinery.com
Address: 20 N. 2nd Avenue, Walla Walla, WA 99362
Phone: (509) 525-9084

HISTORY

Maison Bleue is dedicated to the production of terroir-driven wines from the Walla Walla Valley with an uncompromised style of traditional winemaking techniques, gentle handling and a modest use of French oak. Since the founding in 2007, Winemaker Jon Meuret has produced some of the highest-scoring wines in Washington.

OWNERSHIP & MANAGEMENT

Jon Meuret graduated from the University of Kansas with a Bachelor's of Science in Biology and Chemistry and later completed a Doctorate of Dental Surgery at the University of Iowa. While practicing Dentistry in the Kansas City area, he helped establish a vineyard and winery dedicated to the growing and production of vinifera varieties. It was during this time that Jon decided to make the transition from dentist to full-time vigneron. After completing numerous viticulture and enology courses through University of California, Davis and Washington State University, it was time to chase that dream. Early on, Jon fell in love with wines from the burgeoning wine regions of Oregon and Washington. After many trips to the Pacific Northwest, he and his wife Amy made the move west, settling in Walla Walla, Washington.

In 2015, Jon Meuret partnered with Willamette Valley Vineyards to make Pambrun Wines, named in honor of Pierre Pambrun, Walla Walla's first citizen and Willamette Valley Vineyards' Founder Jim Bernau's fourth great-grandfather. Pambrun Wines are sourced from Seven Hills and Summit View Vineyards and feature small lots of Merlot, Cabernet Sauvignon and a red blend called Chrysologue. Jon Meuret is now the head winemaker for both brands which are jointly showcased in the downtown Walla Walla Tasting Room.

partner in these endeavors while also pursuing a career as a professional artist. Since 1978 Debra's work has been included in numerous solo and group exhibitions in the United States and abroad. For many years Debra taught art as a Visiting Assistant Professor at Cornell University, Ithaca College and Hobart and William Smith Colleges. Her work is included in many public and private collections.

VINEYARD

The winery owns 36 acres of land, out of which 5 acres are under vine. The Walla Walla Valley was carefully selected as the location for Maison Bleue to position it amongst high quality vineyards and grape sources. The vineyards they have selected practice responsible viticulture, ranging from organic to sustainable management. Their style of winemaking focuses on the distinction of these sites as well as achieving true varietal characteristics. They source grapes from Les Colines Vineyard, Seven Hills Vineyard, Waliser Vineyard and Yellow Jacket Vineyard.

Maison Bleue wines are only available at their tasting room and their website.

VISITOR INFORMATION

The winery and tasting room can be visited without appointment. Tastings are available at a cost.

WINES

Voltigeur Viognier

Varietals: Viognier (100%)
Barrel Aging: 11 months in French oak; 40% new
Type of Wine: White
Alcohol: 13,5%
Vintage Year: 2016
Bottle Format: 750ml

Gravière Syrah

Varietals: Syrah (94%), Viognier (6%)
Barrel Aging: 11 months in French oak; 10% new
Type of Wine: Red
Alcohol: 13,7%
Vintage Year: 2016
Bottle Format: 750ml

Voyageur Syrah

Varietals: Syrah (100%)
Barrel Aging: 11 months in French oak
Type of Wine: Red
Alcohol: 13,2%
Vintage Year: 2016
Bottle Format: 750ml

Bourgeois Grenache

Varietals: Cabernet Franc (70%), Merlot (30%)
Type of Wine: Red
Alcohol: 14,9%
Vintage Year: 2014
Bottle Format: 750ml

TINTE CELLARS

Seattle, WASHINGTON

www.tintecellars.com
E-mail: info@tintecellars.com
Address: 19495 – 144th Avenue NE,
Suite A100, Woodinville, WA 98072
Phone: (425) 659-9463

HISTORY

The wineries within Tinte Cellars are pioneers in
the Woodinville Washington warehouse district.
William Church wines reflect a deep commitment
to old world winemaking techniques. They are
intensely terroir-driven and defined by their
subtlety, balance and approachability. Their
award-winning portfolio include a range of robust
reds and much-loved whites, all made with a commitment to minimally invasive techniques.
Cuillin Hills inspired wines embody the pioneering spirit of new world winemaking, focusing
on small lots of highly distinctive wines that are renowned for their creativity, depth and
intensity of character.

OWNERSHIP & MANAGEMENT

For owners Tim Gamble and Teresa Spellman Gamble, Tinte Cellars is the combination of a
love of great wine and a commitment to building strong, inclusive local communities. In
2018, the opportunity arose to purchase two exceptional Woodinville wineries—William
Church and Cuillin Hills. The wineries represented two distinct approaches to Washington

winemaking, but were united by an unrelenting commitment to quality and community. In addition, they were neighbors and collaborators already. Tinte was born, and Tim and Teresa look forward to preserving the legacy of these two great brands, leveraging their track records to forge exciting new wines and new paths for the Tinte brand, its dedicated employees and its valued customers. Tim and Teresa take an active part in running the winery, charting strategic directions and philanthropic opportunities, but have a full-time experienced winemaker and professional staff for daily operations and customer service.

WINEMAKER

A Washington native, Noah Fox Reed was busy earning his degree in Philosophy when he first became interested in wine. He began studying winemaking at Walla Walla Community College, and his passion crystalized when he worked his first harvest in 2003. After stints at a number of wineries, including Chateau Tahbilk in Australia, Noah spent six years as the Assistant Winemaker at Northstar Winery. In 2014, looking for a new challenge and a chance to move back to the west side of the mountains, he took charge of the program at William Church and now masterfully manages winemaking for all of Tinte Cellars' brands.

VINEYARD

Grapes are sourced from several different, highly sought after Washington vineyards, each with their own specific soil compositions. In general, the soils are mostly a silty loam or sandy loam deposited during ice age flooding. As a result of the high sand composition, coupled with cold winter temperatures there has historically been very little nematode pressure. Many vines are own rooted. The soils are very well drained, so irrigation is a necessity given the general lack of rainfall.

Tinte Cellars wines are available at the winery, tasting room and a variety of restaurants and retailers around the region.

Top restaurants that serve Tinte Cellars Wines

1. Barking Frog at Willows Lodge, Woodinville, WA
2. Emory's Lake House, Everett, WA
3. Etta's, Seattle, WA
4. Monsoon, Seattle, WA
5. Pink Door, Seattle, WA
6. Purple Café, Woodinville, WA
7. RN-74, Seattle, WA
8. Ruth's Chris Steak House, Seattle, WA
9. Salt & Iron, Edmonds, WA
10. The Stone House, Redmond, WA

VISITOR INFORMATION

The winery and tasting room can be visited without appointment. Tours and tastings are available at a cost. The winery offers group tours (maximum 25 people) and is also available for private events.

WINES

Viognier

Varietals: Viognier (100%)
Barrel Aging: Stainless steel
Type of Wine: White
Alcohol: 14,1%
Optimal Serving Temperature: 45˚ F
Vintage Year: 2017
Bottle Format: 750ml

Cabernet Sauvignon

Varietals: Cabernet Sauvignon (90%), Petit Verdot
(8%), Cabernet Franc (2%)
Barrel Aging: 20 months in French oak; 48% new
Skin Contact: 15-21 days
Type of Wine: Red
Alcohol: 14,8%
Optimal Serving Temperature: 62˚ F
Vintage Year: 2015
Bottle Format: 750ml

Cabernet Franc

Varietals: Cabernet Franc (100%)
Barrel Aging: 18 months in French oak; 30% new
Skin Contact: 15 days
Type of Wine: Red
Alcohol: 14,5%
Optimal Serving Temperature: 62˚ F
Vintage Year: 2015
Bottle Format: 750ml

Reserve Syrah

Varietals: Syrah (100%)
Barrel Aging: 18 months in French oak; 37% new
Skin Contact: 22 days
Type of Wine: Red
Alcohol: 15,1%
Optimal Serving Temperature: 62˚ F
Vintage Year: 2015
Bottle Format: 750ml

CPSIA information can be obtained
at www.ICGtesting.com
Printed in the USA
LVHW010725190419
614757LV00003B/5